Volkswagen Transporter

Other Titles in the Crowood AutoClassics Series

VOLKSWAGEN TRANSPORTER
The Complete Story

Laurence Meredith

First published in 1998 by
The Crowood Press Ltd
Ramsbury, Marlborough
Wiltshire SN8 2HR

British Library Cataloguing-in-Publication Data
A catalogue record for this book is available from the British
Library.

ISBN 1 86126 159 4

Picture Credits
While the majority of photographs were taken by
Laurence Meredith, the author is grateful to V.A.G. UK Ltd
and Rod Sleigh.

Typeface used: New Century Schoolbook.

Typeset and designed by
D & N Publishing
Membury Business Park, Lambourn Woodlands
Hungerford, Berkshire.

Printed and bound by The Bath Press.

Contents

Evolution

1947   At the Volkswagen factory at Wolfsburg, Dutch VW importer Ben Pon spots a simple truck used for ferrying parts between the assembly lines. Driven by a Beetle engine and based on a Kübelwagen chassis, the truck reminds him of the utility vehicles used by tradesmen in Holland. Pon produces a rough sketch for a VW-based Panelvan.

1949   Major Ivan Hirst (in charge of the running of the Volkswagen factory until the appointment of Heinz Nordhoff as chief executive in January 1948) orders the experimental department to build a prototype transporter.

1950   The first production Panelvans arrive in dealers' showrooms in March. Three months later, production of the Kombi is well under way.

1951   The range-topping Microbus De Luxe, or Samba, is produced; it is unusual in that it has a full-length sunroof, roof 'skylights' and wrap-around rear windows.

1952   Requiring substantial redesign and tooling work, the single-cab Pick-Up arrives, providing the building industry and other trades with a vehicle unrivalled in its ability to withstand abuse.

1953   Engine capacity is increased from 1131cc to 1192cc, and maximum power rises from 25bhp to 30bhp.

1955   The entire range is revised and modernized to include a new fresh-air ventilation system; the cab roof gains its characteristic 'peak'.

1956   Transporter production is transferred from Wolfsburg to Hanover.

1958   The double-cab Pick-Up joins the range.

1961   The high-roof Panelvan, the final model in the range, arrives, and proves almost as popular as its sisters.

1963   The Type 3 saloon's 1500cc engine is offered as an extra-cost option, endowing the Transporter with a welcome increase in power.

1967   After seventeen years in production, the classic Split-Screen buses are replaced by the Bay-Windows. Improvements include more interior space, a 1600cc engine and revised suspension.

1968   Autocratic chief executive Heinz Nordhoff dies suddenly, having successfully steered Volkswagen through some of the company's most difficult days.

1971   Constant criticism from journalists and owners that the Bus is under-powered results in a new twin-carburettor 1700cc engine. Three-speed automatic transmission becomes available as an extra-cost option.

1973   Despite the oil crisis in the Middle East, and the introduction of petrol rationing in some European countries, the cubic capacity of the engine grows to 1800cc.

1975   Apart from introducing the 2-litre engine – the final incarnation of the classic air-cooled flat-four – the company admits in its advertising literature that no further improvements will be forthcoming.

1978   Five four-wheel drive prototypes of the Bay-Window are constructed and tested, but fail to materialize in production.

1979   The Bay-Window range is replaced by the third-generation Wedge – a much larger vehicle, with vastly improved all-round visibility, and other major changes, including a switch from torsion-bar to coil-spring suspension.

1982   In a quest to find more power and reliability, the classic air-cooled engines are replaced by water-cooled petrol and diesel units. The body style remains largely unchanged.

1989   The radically different fourth-generation Transporter is debuted; it has a front-mounted engine driving the front wheels.

Introduction

THE IDEA OF A TRANSPORTER

The classic air-cooled Volkswagen Transporter spans three decades. The different models have consistently outsold their nearest rivals, many times over in some cases, and in its latest incarnation – the fourth-generation front-wheel drive vehicle – the Transporter continues to colonize all four corners of the globe. Volkswagen's 'box on wheels' (as the company's first chief executive Heinz Nordhoff once dubbed it) is probably the only commercial vehicle to have achieved truly classic status in the automobile world.

When the first production Panelvans rolled off the Wolfsburg assembly lines in February 1950, other manufacturers quickly realized that they had been caught on the hop. With a view to exploiting a potentially lucrative market, DKW, Tempo, Ford, Gutbrod, Lloyd, Fiat, Daimler-Benz, and others, all produced variations on the transporter theme.

THE APPEAL OF 'BULLI'

In some cases, the products of other respected manufacturers were more powerful, faster, larger, more spacious and better appointed than Volkswagen's Bus, or 'Bulli' as it is known on the home market, but none was able to equal its overall appeal. The Bus is a truly classless people's *Wagen*, and it is difficult to explain satisfactorily the reasons behind its extraordinary success. Even Volkswagen bosses were sometimes at a loss to understand why their employees had to work a three-shift system around the clock to keep pace with demand. Not that they were complaining.

The first-class dealer network, legendary reliability, exceptional build quality, and an air-cooled engine that was incapable of boiling in summer or freezing in winter – all these features played an important part, yet the Bus always had something more that was quite special.

The war in Vietnam, and the increasing value placed on material goods by Western society, led to the emergence of the Peace movement in North America in the 1960s. The movement adopted the VW Bus as a symbol of the freedom it sought, and the people-carrying Kombis and Microbuses became particularly popular with young people on both sides of the Atlantic. In an attempt to analyse why, the American journal *Car and Driver* published an amusing article in its June 1970 issue. Tom Finn,

The air-cooled Transporters were the world's first multi-purpose vehicles, and the only commercials to gain classic status in their production lifetime.

During the 1960s, the VW Bus was adopted as a symbol of freedom on both sides of the Atlantic by the emerging and powerful Peace Movement.

a 22-year-old Bus owner, and co-chairman of the Leon Trotsky Socialist Purge Committee, wrote:

> A Volkswagen Bus symbolizes freedom. It is perfectly functional; like it is the young American revolutionaries' counterpart to the Russian tractor. Sure, a whole lot of fake cop-out types like the surfers and reactionary college skinheads use them. But among us it means truth and commitment and the right to freak out and get away from the uptight racists who run this country. I mean, man, just give me my Bus, a groovy chick, a jug of Muscatel and a few Reds and I'll put down vibes you wouldn't believe.

For those who were not members of Mr Finn's California-based organization, the Transporter, in its many guises, proved to be a thoroughly practical multi-purpose workhorse. It had almost unrivalled levels of traction, good fuel consumption, and the ability to perform the job for which it was designed for many years after its rivals had been consumed by rust and mechanical maladies. But there was more to it than that.

Above and beyond the Transporter's utilitarian nature, and its capacity to reach 'starship' mileages without incurring serious problems, the real secret of its appeal lay in its look from the front, particularly the Split-Screen model. The circular headlamps, Y-shaped swage lines on the front panel, and curved bumper came together to resemble a humble happy human face, with which people could identify, and which gave a trustworthy and reliable impression.

According to Volkswagen's advertising, the Bus was a family friend who happened to live in the garage rather than in the house. Certainly, this is how many owners came to regard their vehicles. That close relation of the Bus, the Beetle, was the same. In the mid-1960s, when Walt Disney Corporation executives were looking for a suitable vehicle for their first 'Herbie' film, they were able to witness the reaction of the public to the Volkswagen 'face'. They parked a selection of different vehicles, including a Beetle, outside their Hollywood offices. Senior members of the company recorded what happened when members of staff and the public passed by. Crowds frequently gathered around the Beetle, drawn to that happy smiling human face, and hardly gave the other cars a second look.

POST-WAR GERMANY

After the cessation of Second World War hostilities in 1945, motorized transport was in desperately short supply in Germany. Many engineering factories, including Volkswagen's, had been smashed to pieces by successive Allied bombing raids. The first batch of 2,500 production Beetles was assigned to Allied Army personnel, and German civilians had the option either of walking, or of repairing, by whatever means was at their disposal, old and often worn out pre-war machinery. By the end of 1946, even Daimler-Benz had not managed to produce more than 200 vehicles.

It was only after the currency reforms of 1948 that the German economy slowly began to improve. From 1950, the hard work put in by car workers, particularly at Volkswagen's headquarters at Wolfsburg, began to pay off. Transporter owners were to benefit from five years of development of the Beetle. The two vehicles shared many mechanical parts from the factory bins, and faults that afflicted early saloon cars had been eliminated.

Ideally, Volkswagen would have launched a comprehensive range of Buses at the beginning. In fact, owing to a lack of finance, the range was to appear piecemeal over some ten years or so. Investment in new products had to come from profits, and this would take time. There were to be many variations on the basic theme, but basically the range comprised the Panelvan, the Kombi, the Microbus and de luxe Microbus, the single-cab Pick-Up, the wide-bodied Pick-Up, the double-cab Pick-Up, and the high-roof Panelvan. In addition, there were

The key to success: the circular headlamps, Y-shaped swage lines and curved bumper gave the Bus its human 'face'.

ambulances and fire tenders, and a host of tailor-made bodies available to special order. (Incidentally, Volkswagen never produced a Camper; they left others to exploit the leisure market, appointing German specialist coachbuilders Westfalia as 'official' converters.)

German automotive designers have always tended to adopt a conservative, cautious approach to change, and the people at Volkswagen were no exception. Many manufacturers, particularly in America and Britain, would launch new or 'facelifted' models at regular intervals, but the Wolfsburg giant strove only to improve the original designs. Heinz Nordhoff saw change for the sake of change as entirely futile.

Scores of production modifications were made to the Bus through the post-war years. Major changes were announced at the beginning of each new model year, in August, but a good percentage were subcutaneous and went largely unnoticed by journalists and customers alike. An entirely practical man, Nordhoff was influenced most by sales figures when making decisions about new models. It was only when interest in the Split-Screen bus, or 'Splittie' as it is affectionately known, began to decline that Nordhoff instructed the design office to create a suitable replacement.

During the first five years of Splittie production, annual output rose from 8,000 units to nearly 50,000, a phenomenal success by any standards. By 1955, however, this success had brought a few major problems.

Something of a 'watershed' year in Volkswagen lore, 1955 saw Beetle production pass one million. In the same year, the Transporter range was substantially revised, and a superhuman effort had to be made to supply additional chassis and engines to the Karmann concern in Osnabrück, for production of the newly launched two-seater Karmann Ghia sports car. Wolfsburg was bursting at the seams, so a purpose-built factory was constructed at Hanover, and from 1956 all Transporters were made at the new site.

THE CHANGING WORLD

By 1962, when the millionth example was built, the Transporter had been exported to virtually every country in the world. The ruggedness and reliability of the design had proved of equal value on the rough road surfaces of the African continent as on the glass-smooth tarmac of California.

North America was the Transporter's most important export market; in 1963, the 1500 version was launched, and, for a short while, it was only available in the United States. Americans and Canadians, it seemed, just could not get enough of Volkswagens. However, by the mid-1960s, big changes were looming on the horizon. Inspired by the American lawyer, Ralph Nader, consumer groups were becoming seriously concerned with road safety, and by 1967 their concerns had been enshrined in legislation. Almost overnight, motor manufacturers were compelled to focus more carefully on ways in which the threat of serious injury in a road traffic accident could be reduced.

During their seventeen-year production life, the Split-Screen Transporters had endeared themselves to no fewer than 1.8 million people. Now among the most sought-after of all Transporters in the eyes of enthusiasts, the Splittie was simple, relatively crude, and utilitarian in nature. This was part of its charisma and charm, but now the range needed to be replaced – not only because of safety considerations, but for another important reason.

By the mid-1960s, with the emergence of an increasingly expanding middle class, Western society had become more affluent. The demand for inexpensive, austere vehicles

Although North America was always the most important export market, by the mid-1960s, the Bus had colonized the whole globe.

was quickly decreasing. Customers wanted more engine power, greater comfort and increased equipment levels, and they were willing and able to pay for them. This became clear to Volkswagen in 1967, when the company was forced to suspend production of the basic entry-level 1200 Beetle for approximately six months, due to a total lack of demand. Customers bought the more expensive 1300 and 1500 models, despite the German economy having dipped into recession at around this time.

Volkswagen kept abreast with market research. The company knew that if it did not produce exactly what its customers required, another company would. Encouraged by Volkswagen's success with the Transporter, rival manufacturers in Britain, mainland Europe and North Amer-

ica were gaining ground in an expanding market-place with their own multi-purpose vehicles. By the time of the Volkswagen factory's annual shutdown in August 1967, production of the classic Split-Screen Transporter had come to an end. A new era was about to begin.

THE SECOND GENERATION

Although the new 1600cc engine was still positioned at the rear and air-cooled, and the suspension was still by transverse, laminated torsion bars, in most other respects the second generation Bay-Window Bus was built to a wholly fresh design. The range was as comprehensive as before, comprising a Panelvan, a Pick-Up, a Kombi, a Microbus and luxury Microbus (initially dubbed the Clipper), a high-roof Panelvan and a six-seater double-cab Pick-Up. In addition, there was an ambulance and a fire tender, as well as specially equipped models, mostly for use by German public-service utilities. Unlike the Splittie range, the complete Bay range was available right from the beginning of production, in August 1967.

The Bay had a much larger body, squarer styling and a panoramic, one-piece windscreen, and many Splittie die-hards argued, with some conviction, that it lacked the character of the model it replaced. Although they had a valid point, the Bay was correct for a more modern world, and this fact was borne out by the sales figures.

Launched in 1967, the Bay-Window model may have lacked some of the character of the Splittie, but it was correct for the more affluent world of the late 1960s.

A much faster more versatile vehicle, the new model appealed to a wider audience, and, before production ended in 1979, no fewer than 2.5 million units had passed through the dealers' showroom doors. As before, the Panelvan was the most popular model; Westfalia continued to make the 'official' Camper versions.

The Bay had many detail improvements and safety features, the latter to appease and comply with American safety legislation. Some features, like the non-reflecting interior surfaces, were rather pointless – the Split-Screen's painted metal surfaces had never given problems – while others, such as dual-circuit brakes, were to be welcomed.

In their March 1968 road test, *Popular Imported Cars* commented:

> While safety and smog occupy much of the 1968 automotive headline news, appearance, comfort, convenience, handling, ride and utility are additional nouns you can use to describe the new Volkswagen 'boxes', the Beetle's harder-working cousin.

The same report concluded:

> All in all, the 'boxes' have been considerably improved in all the important areas. We leave it to you to decide if beautiful is the word to describe them, but they have got to be driven to be believed.

Volkswagen's engineers and designers believed that beauty and folly usually made good companions, and they were not especially interested in *concours d'élégance* anyway. In the new Transporter range, they had created the world's best cargo- and people-carriers. One journalist after another praised virtually all aspects of the vehicle's design, and many found nothing to criticize until the early 1970s.

Although it was undoubtedly under-powered, even in 2-litre form, the Bay-Window Camper remained popular long after production ceased in 1979.

The 1960s had been a heady decade of massive social upheaval and cultural change. The VW Bus had played an important part in that change and, indeed, in shaping the future. Volkswagen could not, however, afford to become complacent; the threat of serious competition loomed in the east, and the German company could not ignore it.

During the 1970s, recurring criticism from journalists and customers pointed to Volkswagen's stubborn refusal to increase the engine performance of the Bus. With the 1600cc power unit, it was always necessary to shift down a gear or two when lugging uphill. With V8-engined rivals from Detroit, it was not.

In the past, Volkswagen's reluctance to change had been down to Heinz Nordhoff, an old-style dictator who ruled the company with an iron rod. After his death in 1968, Volkswagen was able to be more responsive to criticism and the need to change with the times.

A larger 1700cc engine became available in 1971, an 1800cc in 1973, and a 2-litre by 1975 but, by 1976, the writing was on the wall for the Bay-Windows. Generally acknowledged to have been right first time, the design was gradually improved. Detail production changes were announced as usual at the beginning of each new model year in August but, by the mid-1970s, Volkswagen had no more ideas for improvements, and said so in its advertising. The Bay could be developed no further and the design team, mindful of increasingly stringent legislative demands, came up with a suitable replacement.

CAMPERS CRASH ON

The Camper conversion specialists were never short of ideas. Westfalia in Germany continued as Volkswagen's official converter, but dozens of independent companies, keen to capitalize on a wildly expanding leisure market, sprang up all over the world. Their interior designs were diverse and ingenious. Many Campers were so comprehensively equipped that some people found it possible to live happily all year round in a Bus. Some still do!

As the February 1968 issue of the American publication *Foreign Car Guide* pointed out,

> Volkswagen's Campmobile for 1968 rates as one of the world's fastest quick-change artists – mountain cabin, hunting lodge, fishing camp, seaside cottage or practically any type of resort a vacationing or weekending family could want. About all it takes to work the Campmobile's own sort of magic is a map and the time needed for wander-lusters to drive to their favourite spots. Once at a campsite – either a state or national park or secluded highway miles from nowhere – the Campmobile settles down to carefree use.

Although the Bay-Window had become outdated by 1979, when it was replaced, journalists continued to enthuse about the camping versions. Peter Noad tested an English conversion, the Devon Moonraker, for *VW Safer Motoring* magazine in September 1979, and wrote,

> With several new features, including the new Devon 'Double Top' elevating roof, the 1979 Moonraker is proving to be a best-seller. Notwithstanding the fact that the Type 2 will be replaced next year, Devon have done a good job and if I had the money to spend I would have no hesitation in buying one!

In the Bay-Window, Volkswagen had produced another great classic but, from 1974, sales declined sharply and continued to fall. Beetle sales were also dropping away, and the company found itself in serious trouble.

After the politically engineered oil crisis of 1973, demand for economical, lightweight vehicles prevailed. Japanese manufacturers were only too happy to oblige.

Volkswagen was saved by a new range of front-drive, water-cooled, front-engined cars – the Polo, Scirocco, Golf and Passat. Beetles and Bay-Window Buses had become dinosaurs almost overnight. In its final year of production, the Hanover factory made just 85,632 Buses, in sharp contrast with the 260,000 produced in 1972.

A THIRD GENERATION

For the last of the air-cooled models, the people in the drawing office started with several fresh pieces of paper. They had little option. Nordhoff had once decreed, 'When a box on wheels is the basic need, a box on wheels is the perfect answer.' These famous words were spoken in 1949 and held true for nearly three decades but, by 1979, when the 'Wedge' range of Buses was launched, the developed world had changed out of all recognition.

Greater access to credit had given people a wider choice. Customers were demanding more from their motoring once again, and could afford to pay for it. Along with many other manufacturers, Volkswagen responded to customer demand, and made a policy decision to pitch their products considerably further 'upmarket'. The broad philosophy of a box on wheels still applied, but to a lesser extent than before. If the Splittie had been pretty and the Bay-Window Germanically functional, the Wedge had to be both. It was also required to penetrate the air more efficiently.

In the field of passenger-car design, Citroën was a clear leader in putting aerodynamic theory into practice – at first with its CX model – but Volkswagen was among the first to produce a wind-cheating multi-purpose commercial vehicle. It was a much larger and more stylish vehicle than before, the width of its body increased by a massive 5in (12.5cm) and the length by 2½in (6.25cm). All window glass was also increased in size for enhanced vision and safety, the windscreen by a significant 21 per cent. Both the windscreen and upper part of the front panel were steeply raked, and the panel below the fresh air grille on the front was made more rounded, to allow air to pass over the sides of the vehicle more easily. Fresh and clean, the new body gave more cargo or passenger room and, because the height of the rear panel above the engine lid had been lowered by 5½in (13.75cm), additional luggage space had also been created.

Although built to the same basic construction as Splitties and Bays, this model showed one major departure from conventional Volkswagen thinking. Professor Porsche's famous torsion-bar springing, patented by the Stuttgart office in 1931, was banished to the annals of history. In its place were coil springs and conventional wishbones, cheaper to make, lighter, taking up less space, and easier to manufacture. Another benefit was a smaller turning-circle and (some argued) an improved ride quality, and few owners cared that the coil springs were not as durable.

Interior appointments had improved in the cab to the level of saloon car comfort. Range-topping Microbuses were treated to velour upholstery in place of the Bay-Window's hard-wearing, easy-to-clean vinyl, and rear passengers had more space than ever to stretch their legs. To exploit fully the vastly increased interior volume, Camper specialists were beginning to employ interior designers, who came up with one ingenious layout after another. Equipment levels, accessories and extra-cost options became more diverse; if it had been invented, the converters supplied it. Some vehicles produced by the specialists cost as much to buy as an average three-bedroom house, but there was never a shortage of willing and eager customers.

The third-generation Wedge was still a 'box on wheels', but one in which aerodynamic theory was put into practice for the first time.

Refined, like a car to drive, aesthetically sound, and practical as ever, the entire range suffered from one major drawback. The 2-litre engine and optional 1.6-litre unit were badly under-powered. Fully laden with people, cargo, camping equipment, or a combination of all three, even the 2-litre struggled in comparison with its peers. Both versions would cruise all day at 70mph (110km/h) and more, but acceleration through the gearbox was poor and, on the increasingly congested roads of the late 1970s, overtaking performance in the lower gears counted for more than high cruising speeds. Hammering a Bus, in a quest to keep pace with modern traffic, also had a significant effect on fuel consumption. This is why, in 1980, Volkswagen debuted a conventional 4-cylinder, water-cooled 50bhp diesel engine as an option.

For those who demanded a more powerful petrol engine, the end was in sight by this time for the air-cooled flat-four. Since 1945, the Porsche-designed unit had been refined and developed time and again. The original 25bhp 1131cc engine was eventually bored out to a 1970cc 70bhp unit; after this, Volkswagen deemed its development over.

The engineers could have increased the cubic capacity further, or even added a couple of cylinders, but this would have pushed up the cost to an unacceptable level. To Volkswagen, the solution to a quieter, more fuel-efficient and powerful engine was simple – in place of cooling fins on the outsides of the cast-iron cylinder barrels, there would be cast-alloy water jackets. At the front of the vehicle there would be a large water radiator, and its associated plumbing.

To dyed-in-the-wool 'Volksheads', this move was the ultimate heresy. For Volkswagen, it was the correct commercial decision. For devotees of air-cooled Buses – Splitties, Bays and Wedges – the future lay in the past. The last air-cooled Transporter was made on 31 December 1982.

Many of the 4.8 million who had bought and enjoyed these classic Buses continued to use them, many with even greater enthusiasm. Independent companies on both sides of the Atlantic proliferated, to cater for owners' needs. Spare parts continued to be made available through Volkswagen's dealer network, and those that had 'dried up' were re-manufactured by specialists. Today, most parts for all three generations are plentiful; some are difficult to obtain and expensive, but they are available. This is just one reason why so many VW Buses around the world are being rebuilt and restored, many to the highest attainable standards.

1. Transporter-Generation
1950 bis 1967

2. Transporter-Generation
1967 bis 1979

3. Transporter-Generation
ab August 1979

Three generations of cab interiors, each more comfortable, better appointed and safer than the last.

16

1 VW Transporter: From the Cinders of War

THE REBUILDING OF WOLFSBURG

When the Allies arrived at Wolfsburg in 1945, the Volkswagen factory presented a pitiful sight. Fearful that Hitler had ordered his deadly flying bombs to be made there, the Americans had knocked seven bells out of the building in successive bombing raids. In fact, no evidence was discovered in the battered factory of anything connected with flying bombs. During hostilities, 630 Beetles had been produced, for use by middle- and high-ranking Nazi officers, before the factory had begun to concentrate its efforts on production of the Kübelwagen, stoves to keep German troops warm on the cold Russian front, and other military equipment.

Wolfsburg fell into the British occupation zone, and responsibility for making sense of the mess was given to Major Ivan Hirst of the Royal Electrical and Mechanical Engineers

After successive Allied bombing raids in 1944, much of the factory at Wolfsburg was destroyed.

17

Responsibility for rebuilding the factory and starting Beetle production fell to Major Ivan Hirst (right), of the REME.

(REME). To a lesser man, the task ahead might have seemed impossible. Most of the factory roof had crashed to the floor, there were thousands of PoWs with little to eat, and the raw materials necessary for the resumption of Beetle production were in short supply.

A skilled administrator, gifted linguist and a natural manager of people, Hirst set about reviving the Beetle project with what was available. Coal to fire the blast furnaces was secured from the Russians. Key machine tools, which had been stored in the grounds of the factory, had survived the bombing raids, and Hirst ordered them to be brought back to where they belonged. Working long hours, Hirst and his team were able to start producing Beetles, and by 1946, 10,000 cars had been made. Crude as they were, they provided much-needed transport. Working in conditions that would be considered wholly unacceptable today,

A truck like this, used for internal transport at Wolfsburg, gave Dutchman Ben Pon the idea for the first Panelvan.

An unsung hero of the twentieth century, Ivan Hirst lives quietly in retirement in his native Yorkshire.

Hirst's team gradually rebuilt the factory and stepped up Beetle production. In 1947, the first exports were made to Holland.

BEN PON'S IDEA

The official Dutch importer, Ben Pon, was the first to put forward the idea for the Transporter, or Type 2, as it was officially designated in the drawing office. Like Hirst, Ben Pon was a motoring man through and through, with a deep appreciation and understanding of automobiles. Indeed, both Pon and Hirst had owned and driven many thoroughbred sports machines; they understood each other well, and had a great deal in common.

On one of his many visits to the Wolfsburg factory in 1947, Pon spotted several trucks being used for carrying Beetle parts from one

assembly line to another. Simply constructed with a Kübelwagen chassis, flat bed, Beetle running gear and a small cab, these trucks – one of which was still recently in use at the factory – served as the factory's only means of internal mechanized transport and played a vital role in production.

In Pon's eyes, these trucks were not simply crude load-luggers; it occurred to him that in principle they might provide the basis for something considerably more useful. They reminded him of the small trades' vehicles with which he was familiar in his home country, but they were slow, inefficient, and could only carry small loads. Pon took a scrap of paper and a pencil, and sketched the outline of a cargo van. The drawing is hardly a work of art – it might have done by an unwilling schoolboy – but it bears an uncanny resemblance to what eventually became the Split-Screen Panelvan.

Pon showed his drawing to Ivan Hirst and discussed his proposal with him, insisting that a production vehicle could easily become a success. Although he remained typically reserved, the British Army officer did agree that there was an urgent need for a commercial vehicle. A conquered nation struggling to find its feet, and resume internal and external trading links, would find many uses for a practical, reliable vehicle for transporting goods and people.

If it had been left to Hirst, the project would have been started immediately, but he and Pon had first to overcome a major stumbling block. Colonel Charles Radclyffe, for whom Hirst had the utmost respect, was in overall charge of light engineering in the British occupied zone. Radclyffe's permission was required for all new projects requiring additional manpower and resources. He was a patient and reasonable man, but he always erred on the side of caution. He listened with great interest to Pon's proposal for the new commercial vehicle, agreed that the idea was a good one, but concluded that it was impracticable. He argued that the factory workers were already overstretched, producing Beetles, as were the various outside suppliers of components, such as Bosch, SWF, Solex and Ambi Budd. Radclyffe was right. To have asked more of the workers at this stage would have been unreasonable, if not impossible.

Pon and Hirst were disappointed, but Hirst was a canny and resourceful Yorkshireman, and believed in finding a way where there was a will.

THE APPOINTMENT OF HEINZ NORDHOFF

By the end of 1947, the traumas of the early days after Germany's surrender were all but over. The British Army was still overseeing the Wolfsburg factory, but could not remain in charge for ever. Hirst and his team had been instrumental in helping the Germans shape their economic destiny, but the time was quickly coming for the British to take a back seat. It was inevitable that a German would have to be appointed as chief

One of eight prototypes, this Panelvan is without a rear window and bumper, and has the fuel filler on the outside; the huge engine lid – which led to the 'Barndoor' nickname – characterized the first five years of the vehicle's production.

executive of Volkswagen, to steer the company in the right direction, towards a profitable future. On Hirst's recommendation, ex-Opel manager Heinz Nordhoff took up the post from 1 January 1948.

Nordhoff was widely regarded as the best man for the job, but, although Hirst and he got along all right at arm's length, the Englishman was one of many who disliked him. Being liked was not what Nordhoff was to be paid for. Like Hirst, Nordhoff was a natural manager of people, but his autocratic, dictatorial methods were wholly different.

Throughout 1948, Beetle exports increased. A number of car dealers in other European countries began to see the financial potential of the little car, and, although it would be another four or five years before the lucrative British and North American markets could be attacked, profits were being made and reinvested for the future. At this point, Pon's idea for a new commercial vehicle was slowly resurrected, and Nordhoff responded to it positively.

THE BUS PROTOTYPES

These days, motor manufacturers spend millions of dollars and an average of four years developing a new vehicle. In the late 1940s, bureaucracy, legislative demands, and conflicting results of market research projects, simply did not exist. When Nordhoff – the typically straight-talking German – instructed the drawing office to design a 'box on wheels', he meant just that. It would not take long; a child of five could draw a box on wheels in less than two minutes, but Volkswagen's draughtsmen were given the luxury of a few weeks.

Inevitably, the design was centred around as many Beetle components as possible, in order to keep production costs down. To this end, the 1131cc 25bhp air-cooled engine was

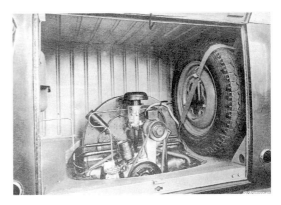

An early brochure picture shows the diminutive 1131cc 25bhp engine with its single Solex carburettor, vertical fan housing and cast-alloy dynamo pedestal.

installed at the rear, and the four-speed non-synchromesh gearbox was bolted directly to it. Largely constructed of aluminium-alloy, the horizontally opposed, 4-cylinder engine was exceptionally light and easy to maintain.

Engine

The short crankshaft ran in three main bearings, with a fourth to support the auxiliary drives. A single camshaft sat below the crankshaft, was driven from the latter by helical gears, and operated the overhead valves by pushrods and rockers. The alloy crankcase was made in two pieces, split vertically down the centreline and bolted together. The crankcase halves, incidentally, were made in matching pairs.

Supplied by Mahle, the alloy pistons were flat-topped, and ran inside cast-iron cylinder barrels, finned on the outside to reduce weight and aid cooling. The two alloy cylinder heads were secured to the outside of the barrels with long threaded studs, which ran directly through the barrels to each half of the crankcase.

In the long-term interests of reliability, the unit was intentionally understressed.

Pre-launch publicity material promised a Kombi version with windows, coarse floor carpeting, and easily detachable seats.

Initially, the simple Solex 26VFI carburettor served the wedge-shaped combustion chambers through an inlet manifold of a very small diameter; valve diameter was restricted to a diminutive 28.6mm for both the inlet and exhaust.

With a bore and stroke of 75 × 64mm, power output from the original 1131cc engine was no more than 25bhp at 3,300rpm. Because of fluctuations in the quality of fuel during the early days throughout the whole of Europe, the compression ratio was kept low, at 5.8:1.

Cooling was taken care of by a fan vertically mounted in the fan housing bolted to the top of the crankcase. The fan was driven by the dynamo, which in turn was belt-driven from the crankshaft pulley wheel. Cold air

drawn from outside was blown over the cylinder heads, barrels and vertical oil cooler, which was also mounted in the fan housing on the left-hand side of the crankcase. To prevent hot spent air re-entering the engine bay and causing overheating, cooling trays were placed over the cylinder barrels and sealed with rubber on their outer edges. There was no separate sump, the oil being contained 'at rest' in the bottom of the crankcase. A conventional gear-driven oil pump housed at the rear of the engine drove lubricant through holes drilled in the crankshaft, journals and pushrods for 'top end' lubrication.

From the engine bay there was little to see of the power unit itself; here there was an 8.8-gallon (40-litre) fuel tank housed on the left-hand side, the 6-volt battery on the right, and the spare wheel horizontally disposed on a shelf above the engine. Engine ancillaries within easy reach for maintenance were the coil, bolted to the left-hand side of the fan housing, the oil bath air cleaner above the carburettor, the mechanical fuel pump and Bosch distributor, both secured to the left-hand crankcase half, and the dynamo, which sat on a pedestal cast as an integral part of the right-hand crankcase.

Engine removal was made easier by the detachable valance, secured to the bodywork with bolts. The engine was mated to the gearbox with just four bolts. A pure Beetle unit, the original non-synchromesh gearbox had a ribbed alloy casing in two pieces split vertically and, like the engine, bolted together down the centreline.

Drive was taken up by a cable-operated single dry-plate Fichtel & Sachs clutch, positioned in the bellhousing of the gearbox. The crownwheel and pinion were located in the gearbox towards the rear, the two driveshafts, or swing axles, running in hollow axle tubes through fulcrum plates on their inner ends, and to hub reduction gearboxes on their outer ends.

The Panelvan first appeared in 1950 and was always the staple of the range. Until March 1955, the Bus was without the 'peak' above the windscreen. Note that the engine cooling louvres are cut to face 'outwards' at this stage.

'Barndoors' had small tail-lamps, a single brake light in the centre of the engine lid, and a narrow window at the top. Rear bumpers were an extra-cost option from 1953.

Suspension

Suspension at the rear was by transverse torsion bars housed in tubes in front of the gearbox, parallel trailing arms bolted to the outer ends of the torsion tubes at the front, and to the driveshaft tubes at the rear. Damping was by double acting telescopic shock absorbers. The front suspension was also by torsion bars housed in two transverse tubes, situated one above the other, twin parallel trailing arms and telescopic dampers.

The suspension was, of course, independently sprung at all four corners at a time when solid rear axles and cart springs were the norm on commercial vehicles. It was innovative, tried and tested on the Beetle and the wartime Kübelwagen before being

Plain, unadorned bodywork, a strong wrap-around bumper and 16in wheels shod with crossply tyres were all part of this utility package. Note the large VW emblem in the centre of the hubcaps, highlighted in black.

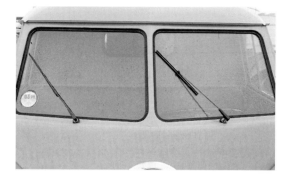

A pre-war relic, the metal division between the two halves of the windscreen led to the universal 'Splittie' name.

With so much sheet metal, the Panelvan lent itself particularly well to the art of the signwriter.

adopted by the Transporter, but was dogged by one major drawback.

The supposed vagaries of the rear swing-axle system were perceived by some to be potentially dangerous – although not at first – but they were grossly misunderstood by the press and public. A tendency for the swing axles to 'jack themselves up' and adopt wheel 'tuck-under' was an inherent characteristic of the design. However, the speed at which this would occur is way beyond the bravery and skill of most drivers; in many years of trying hard, I have never achieved back-end break-away or wheel tuck-under in a Split-Screen Bus. The criticism levelled against this system during the 1960s by Ralph Nader and others is largely academic.

Steering and Brakes

The steering gear design was based on the Beetle principle, with a worm and peg steering gearbox, unequal length tie rods and articulation of the brake drums by king and link pins. A steering damper wasn't fitted until March 1955, its advantages being instantly felt and appreciated.

Hydraulically operated drum brakes were used all round; the luxury of discs at the front did not arrive until 1970. Two leading shoes were fitted at the front, while the rears had one leading and one trailing shoe. Each drum was 9.06in (230mm) in diameter and similar to the Beetle's, except that the front drums were made stronger from 1953.

Body and Chassis

For the first prototype, the large 'no frills' Panelvan body was bolted directly to a standard Beetle chassis complete with torsion bars and running gear. A Panelvan body, or even a variety of different bodies, fitted to the Beetle chassis, would have been convenient from a manufacturing point of view, but, unfortunately, things were not so simple. 'If only everything in life was as reliable as a Volkswagen.'

Second Thoughts

The first prototype was up and running in a very short time. It proved in testing to be a complete disaster. Despite the inherent strength of the Beetle's backbone chassis, it was not up to the job, and twisted and folded up under the weight of the Transporter body. Nordhoff and his designers had little option but to return immediately to the drawing board. It was time to apply fundamental mathematical principles in designing a new chassis, in place of the wishful thinking that had been a feature of the first effort.

Subsequent prototypes were considerably stronger. The Beetle's engine, torsion bar suspension and running gear were all retained, but the new body/chassis unit was, to all intents and purposes, of the unitary construction type. Two sturdy longitudinal

The Kombi was the entry-level people carrier, a Panelvan with windows and removable seats. This American-spec vehicle has 'bullet-type' indicators with clear lenses, and sealed-beam headlamps.

box section pieces running the entire length of the body were strengthened by crossmembers; outriggers welded to the outsides of the main longitudinals supported the outer parts of the body. The steel floors in the cab, cargo area and rear luggage bay above the engine were welded directly to this frame, making for a solid integral unit. The result was an extremely strong structure, resistant to twisting and bending in all driving conditions, even when overloaded.

At this stage, the Transporter successfully challenged contemporary design thinking. At the time, there was no truck or van that was not built to a front-engined, rear-wheel drive layout. This layout was fine with a full load on board, but it was different when the vehicle was empty. As Heinz Nordhoff once pointed out, the state of the

trees that lined the roads in and out of Wolfsburg was a good indication of the way British Army trucks handled without a load on board, especially in wet weather.

With the engine and gearbox at the rear, driver and two passengers in the cab and the load – up to three-quarters of a ton – confined to the centre section, weight distribution was almost perfect front to rear. The great advantage of this layout was that the balance was maintained, even without a load. Where handling and roadholding are concerned, it could be argued that no one has ever improved upon the theory of the design.

Towards Production

Throughout the latter half of 1949, the prototypes, eight in total, were severely tested

A roll-top sunroof, roof skylights, bright trim, 'full-width' dashboard and two-tone paintwork distinguished the range-topping Samba from the other models.

Volkswagen's Brazilian plant also made Buses, which served particularly well as taxis.

over thousands of miles. Germany's roads was so appalling at the time that a weakness in any component would have quickly shown itself. Generally, the test vehicles coped with the punishment well, but changes were required between the first and subsequent prototypes. The front body panel was made more curved, resulting in the clutch, brake and throttle pedals being spaced more comfortably. Both the front axle tubes and dampers were strengthened, and braking performance was improved.

Detail changes included re-profiled cab seats, for improved comfort, the addition of

Debuted in 1952, the single-cab Pick-Up required major modifications, including new pressings for the roof panel, bed flaps and locker-bed door, a flatter fuel tank, and a 'cut-down' engine lid; it proved especially popular with the building trade.

The six-seater double-cab Pick-Up, fitted here with the optional tarpaulin and bows, was added to the range in 1958. This immaculate 1964 example is owned by American enthusiast Bruce Jones, from Atlanta, Georgia.

opening hinged doors on the side of the body, to aid access to the load area – sliding doors would have been more useful – and an enlarged luggage space above the engine. The fuel filler was moved, from its position high up on the outside of the left rear quarter of the bodywork, to the inside of the engine bay. This was a rather quaint security measure, taken because fuel theft by siphoning was not entirely unknown in post-war Germany!

By far the most important problem the experimental office had to address was the vehicle's sluggish acceleration when fully laden. Today, they would probably have bolted a turbocharger to the engine, but such a luxury was not available to the engineers at that time. Instead, the designers drew on the genius of Professor Porsche, and fitted reduction gears in the rear hubs, a trick that 'the old man' had employed on the Kübelwagens nearly ten years before. It provided an inexpensive solution to what was ostensibly an expensive problem. Curiously, the reduction gears were employed on all Splitties, right up until the end of production in 1967.

One modification suggested by Nordhoff concerned the cab seat. The designers had come up with a three-man bench seat, but Nordhoff considered that a two-man bench and a separate driver's seat would be a more appropriate arrangement. He was politely informed that this was not technically possible, and invited to concern himself with running the company, rather than poking his nose into affairs that did not concern him.

Nordhoff's idea was sound, if only because the driver's seat could have been made adjustable, but the designers were adamant that it could not be done. In characteristic style, Nordhoff would get his way, but it would be another twelve years before the mysteries of a separate seat were unravelled.

With a top speed of 50mph (80km/h), the Transporter was hardly a contender for pole position in the Le Mans 24-Hours, but it had a cargo volume of 162cu ft, could carry its own weight between its axles, and would travel for well in excess of 100,000 miles (160,000km) without requiring major surgery to the engine, and withstand use and abuse beyond that which anyone might deem to be reasonable.

The eight prototypes produced in 1949 comprised six Panelvans, a Kombi (with seats and windows) and a Microbus, with a more luxuriously appointed interior. They all acquitted themselves beyond expectation and, on 12 November 1949, the first Transporter was shown to journalists. The vehicle was well received, with the majority of motoring writers praising it for its driveability, good fuel consumption, and surprisingly good performance.

Tooling and gearing up for production took most of the winter, and the first production Panelvans were not available in dealers' showrooms until March 1950. The people-carrying Kombi arrived three months later.

A final addition to the Splittie range for 1962, the high-roof Panelvan was a versatile load carrier; because of its extra headroom, it saw service in all sorts of unlikely roles.

Heinz Nordhoff (right) proudly announces the 100,000th Transporter, on 9 October 1954. Within less than two years, the range would be modernized and production transferred from Wolfsburg to Hanover.

The Press Paves the Way

To launch a vehicle as crude and simple as the early Volkswagen Panelvan today would surely lead quickly to bankruptcy, but in 1950 it created a true sensation. Nothing like it had ever been seen before. Before trying the Panelvan for the first time, all the motoring journalists had preconceived notions about commercial vehicles. After all, the average truck or van, whether built in America or Europe, was a noisy, uncomfortable, diesel-engined monster capable of little more than 40mph (64km/h), and with little in the way of stopping power.

One journalist after another heaped praise on Volkswagen's new vehicle, and one or two even took the trouble to warn Detroit seriously to think again. *Cars Illustrated of America* called it 'the second automobile revolution since the Beetle'. *Transport and Technology* magazine commented,

> The outstanding handling characteristics of the passenger car, such as suspension, roadholding and acceleration, have been transposed to the eight-seater Bus version. This allows suspension settings that are simply not attainable with varying weights on the axles, and also results in fully even use of the tires' carrying ability and brakes.

What surprised most was the Bus's car-like driving qualities; the steering was pleasantly light, the brake and clutch pedals required minimal foot pressure, and the high-up driving position gave a commanding view of the road ahead. Good roadholding and driver safety were high on *Auto Motor und Sport*'s list of priorities.

In the early days, members of the press found little to criticize in the Bus; they even excused the absence of a dashboard and fuel gauge, on the grounds that commercial vehicles did not really need such 'luxuries'. While it is true to say that, during the 1950s, many of the leading motoring writers did not risk criticizing manufacturers' products, for fear of missing out on the next all-expenses-paid trip abroad, in the case of the Bus, their positive response was about right. Their opinion was endorsed by the increasing number of customers who queued at dealers' showrooms to purchase the new Transporter.

Major Ivan Hirst: An officer and a gentleman

Now in his eighties and living quietly in retirement in his native rural Yorkshire, Ivan Hirst is one of the unsung heroes of the twentieth century. Without his considerable skill and effort, neither the Transporter nor the Beetle would have come into being. Modest and unassuming, Hirst possesses rare human qualities. A true gentleman, he retains the morals and values of past generations, enjoys the physical fitness of a man half his age, and has the mental clarity of a newly qualified doctor of jurisprudence. For him, the British Army is a distant memory, but one over which he has instant recall.

A gifted linguist, skilled administrator and a great motivator of men, Hirst listened attentively to Ben Pon's idea for a production Panelvan, and was eventually to push resources to the limit to ensure that the project went into production. Today, Hirst accepts little credit for his achievements, but he is still held in the highest regard by Volkswagen's top brass, both in Germany and Britain. Senior personnel continue to visit him on a regular basis.

In the mid-1980s, Volkswagen invited Hirst and his late wife to attend an important meeting in Wolfsburg, despatching a Lear jet to carry them to and from the venue. It is typical of Hirst that he felt a little uncomfortable aboard this luxury aircraft, because he was unsure whether modern etiquette required him to offer a tip to the pilot or not. In Wolfsburg, Hirst met up with an old chum, Ferry Porsche. After some time, a gleaming black, chauffeur-driven Porsche 911 turbo pulled up outside the factory. Ferry Porsche politely excused himself and climbed into the passenger seat of the 911, its engine running, its chauffeur ready to go. Porsche was due back in Stuttgart for an important board meeting. The chauffeur had been given strict instructions about the merit of punctuality, and, as soon as Ferry had strapped himself in, he let the clutch pedal out and left two long lines of rubber on the road all the way to the factory gates and beyond.

In the small village near Huddersfield where he now lives, Major Hirst is known locally as Ivan, the kind, softly spoken, pipe-smoking gentleman who drives a Golf GTi. If anyone addresses him as 'Sir', a title that many argue should have been officially bestowed upon him years ago, they are instantly rebuked. 'My name is Ivan,' he says. 'All that "Sir" nonsense finished a long time ago.'

The Transporter was, according to Hirst, absolutely essential in getting Germany back to normal. 'We had to build it, by hook or crook,' he says. 'It was simply that Ben Pon was right; trades people needed transport for carrying tools and equipment. Restoring Germany's infrastructure after the War wasn't easy and naturally took quite some time, but the Transporter was eventually to play a vital role in the restoration of the country's economy.'

Hirst remained at Wolfsburg until the early 1950s, to 'keep an eye on things'. Once Heinz Nordhoff had demonstrated that he was the right man to run the company, Hirst left Volkswagen, and

Major Ivan Hirst: An officer and a gentleman *continued*

took up a post as an international translator with the OECD in Paris. On his departure, he was presented with a brand-new Beetle Cabriolet, in recognition of his efforts. As an army officer, he could not accept gifts and politely declined it. Volkswagen insisted that he at least accept a scale model of a Beetle, one of a batch of four. One was given to Adolf Hitler, one to Porsche in Stuttgart, and one to Bosch. The Bosch model was sold at auction in Britain in 1996 for £42,500, but Hirst's, which he still has, is destined for a military museum.

Hirst looks back fondly on the time that he spent helping to shape the Volkswagen concern. He did not design either the Transporter or the Beetle, but he did make both happen, and against the odds. Industry experts in Britain and the United States had dismissed the Volkswagen as unviable. After the war, engineers working for the Rootes Group in Britain dismantled a Kübelwagen and published a paper about it. They pointed out that it had some interesting technical points, but concluded that a rear-engined air-cooled vehicle would never catch on. A lesser man than Ivan Hirst might have capitulated and agreed with them. But he did not. Hirst strongly believed in picking up the pieces after a war that had destroyed so much. He succeeded where others considered the task to be too difficult.

To be an Army Major who survived the Second World War, who enjoys a 'tipple' and a regular intake of tobacco smoke, and is still going strong at over 80 years of age, is a remarkable feat. But to have also ensured that the two most significant vehicles of the twentieth century went into production in almost impossible circumstances is an achievement without parallel in the motor industry.

2   The Split-Screen Range

THE PANELVAN

Exterior

Nicknamed the 'barn door', after its exceptionally large, top-hinged engine lid, the early Panelvan was austere and basic in its appointments. It even lacked a rear window until April 1951, and the rear bumper was conspicuous by its absence until March 1953, when one became available as an extra-cost option. By today's standards, the vehicle's appearance was drab, to say the least. Chromium-plated trim was minimal, confined to the bezels around the headlamps and tail-lamps, and the door and engine-lid handles. A single brake light was housed separately in the middle of the barn door, above the registration plate. Engine-cooling louvres were cut into the side body panels above the wheel arches, and further ones featured higher up close to the roof, to ventilate the load area.

Supplied by SWF, the semaphore indicators were positioned in the bodywork behind the cab doors and operated by solenoids. A large V-over-W roundel on the front panel between the headlamps, and in the centre of the painted hubcaps, identified the vehicle as a Volkswagen, but badging was otherwise absent. The 16in road wheels were to the usual Volkswagen/Porsche five-bolt design; similar wheels were employed on the Beetle, Porsche 356 and Porsche farm tractors. With a width of 3in and shod

Sweeping changes were made across the board from March 1955. At the front, the styling was improved by the peak over the windscreen, which, with two grilles on its underside, allowed for improved cabin ventilation.

with narrow Continental crossply tyres, the excellent roadholding properties commended by contemporary journalists must be regarded as comparative and relative.

Inside the Cab

The cab, separated from the load area by a steel panel with an integral window, also provided the basics, but with one or two surprising exceptions. Following the example

A 'full-width' dashboard was no longer confined to the Samba, but extended across the range. The fresh-air collection and distribution box is in the centre of the roof panel. The property of Steve Saunders, this Bus also has a lamp fitted to the windscreen for reading signposts at night.

of the standard version of the Beetle, rather than the de luxe or export version, there was a large three-spoke steering wheel, a large boxy binnacle directly in front of the steering column, housing a single instrument – the speedometer – and a plain vinyl-covered bench seat.

Calibrated to 80km/h (50mph), the speedometer had a needle that appeared to run backwards, a feature common in pre-war vehicles, but less so by the early 1950s. The headlamp beam, semaphore indicators, dynamo charge and oil-pressure warning lights were placed around the speedometer on the binnacle. A simple toggle switch on top of the dashboard operated the indicators.

The interior cab door panels, made of a crude compressed fibreboard material, had small stowage bins cut into them, and ribbed rubber mats covered the floor. The cab offered a no-frills package, as ergonomically sound as a torture rack; the firmly sprung seats were very hard, but a heater, and swivelling quarter lights in the cab door windows for ventilation, were provided as standard. A heater was by no means standard in all passenger cars at this time, let alone in commercial vehicles, but it was one of the many advantages of the air-cooled engine. Hot air produced by the engine and exhaust pipes was ducted through heater boxes positioned at the front of the exhausts, and channelled 'at no extra cost' through into the cab, for warmth and windscreen de-misting. The flow of heat could be controlled by a revolving tap next to the choke button roughly in the centre of the cab floor, close to the base of the seat squab.

On discovering the existence of a heater, Laurence J. Cotton, writing in *Commercial*, commented,

> This I found to be most effective within a few minutes of starting the engine, and the only possible fault that could be visualized is that fumes are prone to emanate from an engine that has seen considerable service and might also be forced into the cab. As it is, Volkswagen has provided an effective unit without additional cost.

Seat belts were not fitted, but passengers were encouraged by a sense of self-preservation to steady themselves with a footbar and grab handle in the unfortunate event of an accident.

Carrying

With the exception of the 'stepped' panel that formed the floor of the luggage compartment above the engine, the cargo floor was completely flat, each panel that made up the floor being corrugated for extra strength. With a payload space of 141cu ft in the main centre section and an additional 21cu ft over the engine bay, the Transporter boasted virtually unrivalled carrying capacity.

Power and Performance

A number of journalists who tested the early vehicles considered that the comparatively good pulling power of the engine led to the temptation to overload the vehicle

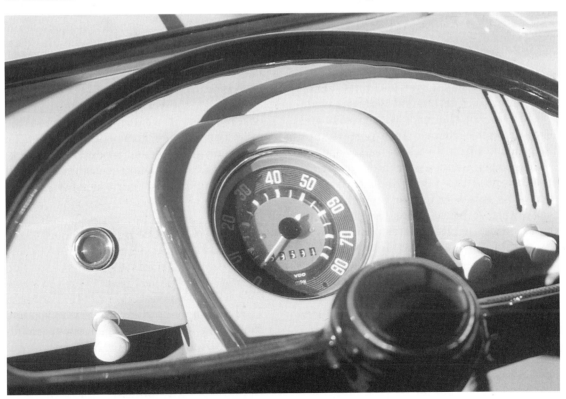

Another March 1955 change was from a three- to a two-spoke steering wheel, and the adoption of a more modern-looking speedometer.

The Samba's dashboard was the same as that on the regular models, except for the clock on the passenger's side.

beyond its three-quarter-ton limit. They were right, too. Commercial operators could often be seen on the roads with grossly and illegally over-burdened Transporters, but the good old Bus always seemed to cope.

Volkswagen claimed that the Transporter would climb a 1 in 4.3 gradient with a full load. This was a tall order for 25bhp and many were sceptical about the claim, but the Bus acquitted itself in tests, and proved the manufacturers correct in their claim time and again. Abuse of the clutch was required in stop-start manoeuvres on such steep gradients, but it rarely failed to live up to its quickly gained reputation as the toughest commercial around.

Cruising at a steady 50mph (80km/h) – its top and maximum cruising speed – with a full load on board, fuel consumption turned out at around 30mpg (9.43l/100km). Around town this figure could swiftly drop to below 20mpg (14.15l/100km), but owners still rated the

Bus highly competitive and fuel-efficient in comparison with contemporary commercials.

Gearbox

Early criticism, which came from owners rather than journalists, was centred around the 'crash' gearbox. For many, the Panelvan was their first means of mechanized transport – not an ideal introduction to driving – and coping with the demands of double-declutching and silent shifting often proved too much. Each journey was characterized by the most cruel 'scrunching' and scraping of the gear wheel teeth. The owners of the pre-1952 Porsche 356s, also fitted with a crash box, made similar complaints to senior management in Stuttgart.

Volkswagen came to the rescue of Bus owners in March 1953 with the introduction of synchromesh on second, third and top gears. An all-new gearbox with synchromesh on all four forward speeds (*see* page 51) arrived in May 1959.

Although the versatility of the Panelvan ensured that it would always remain the most popular and best-selling Volkswagen commercial throughout production, it quickly became obvious that the design lent itself easily to a number of variations on a theme.

THE FIRST PEOPLE CARRIERS

The Kombi and the Microbus

The Kombi and the Microbus debuted in June 1950. They were built to the same mechanical specification as the Panelvan, the most obvious differences being the three rectangular windows on each side of the bodywork, and seats in the cargo area. Constructed with tubular steel frames and plain vinyl upholstery, these seats in the rear passenger area

Split-Screen Volkswagen Transporter 1950–67

Specification
Body type	Panelvan, Pick-Up, Kombi, Microbus, wide-bodied Pick-Up, double-cab Pick-Up, high-roof Panelvan
Chassis	Ladder-type chassis frame welded integrally with the body

Engine
Type	Horizontally-opposed four cylinder
Capacity	1131cc
Bore	75mm
Stroke	64mm
Compression ratio	5.8:1
Cylinders	Detachable cast-iron, finned barrels bolted to an alloy crankcase
Cylinder heads	Made of light alloy with two valves per cylinder operated by a single camshaft, pushrods and rockers
Maximum power	25bhp at 3,300rpm
Maximum torque	67Nm at 2,000rpm

Gears
Gearbox type	Four-speed manual without synchromesh until 1953
Gear ratios	First 3.60:1, Second 2.07:1, Third 1.25:1, Fourth 0.81:1, Reverse 6.60:1
Clutch	Fichtel & Sachs single dry-plate

Suspension, brakes and steering
Front suspension	Transverse torsion bars, parallel trailing arms and telescopic dampers
Rear suspension	Transverse torsion bars, trailing arms, telescopic dampers and swinging half axles
Brakes	Cast-iron drums
Steering	Worm and peg, unequal length tie rods, king and link pins
Wheels and tyres	16in diameter steel road wheels, 5.60 × 16 Continental crossply tyres

Dimensions
Overall length	159in (403.75cm)
Overall width	66in (167.5cm)
Overall height	73.5in (186.88cm)
Wheelbase	94.5in (240cm)
Track	52.6in (133.75cm)
Ground clearance unladen	18.75in (47.5cm)
Fuel tank capacity	8.8 gallons (40 litres)
Unladen weight	18cwt (914kg)

Performance
Maximum speed	50mph (80km/h)
0–40mph (0–65km/h)	22.7secs
Fuel consumption	Approximately 25mpg (11.32l/100km)

At the rear, the 'barndoor' was replaced by a top-hinged tailgate and a separate, much smaller engine lid.

were attached to the floor with butterfly nuts and could be removed in a matter of minutes, allowing the Kombi to double as a cargo carrier. This was the entry-level people Transporter, a truly versatile piece of equipment.

Many people-carrying Buses were quickly pressed into service all over Europe as taxis and school buses, and as multi-purpose family leisure vehicles. The upmarket Microbus, with its fixed seats and improved level of trim, reflected the first signs of post-war German affluence.

One of the principal differences between the Panelvan and the people-carrying Buses was that the people carriers did not have the full dividing wall between the cab and centre passenger section. Instead, there was a cut-down panel, which, on certain models after 1953, could be specified with a walkway through to the cab.

Interior Décor

With both the Kombi and the Panelvan, Volkswagen aimed to provide simple utility vehicles that performed admirably in the transport of people and goods. The company's policy was to charge extra for items that were not deemed strictly necessary. (This policy is still followed to a certain extent in the German motor industry today.) Rubber mats were fitted to the cab floor across the range as a matter of course, but the Panelvan possessed no such luxury in the cargo area. The Kombi got a mat in the cargo-cum-passenger area.

Both models were without a headlining and interior panelling. Painted metal panels were rather uninspiring aesthetically, so those with extra cash bought a Microbus, which had a headlining in soft cloth and vinyl-covered interior panels decorated with strips of bright trim. This 'decadence' was hardly luxurious by today's standards, but the additional trim had the added advantage of absorbing mechanical noise from the engine and transmission, making the passengers' ride much quieter.

Reviews and Test Drives

As austere as the Kombi was, journalists continued to enthuse about it for many years. The American magazine *Mechanix* commented:

> The greatest in the world would be one way of describing the Volkswagen station wagon if there was anything around to compare it with. Actually, it's strictly a one-of-a-kind deal, liked striped hair or a six-legged horse. It is the only station wagon I have ever seen that has enough up-and-down room and forward-and-aft space to take the station with you – if you want to.

This little beetle can carry eight people with ease to the 8.15 train, and all their luggage for a world cruise. The big deal, and why we're bringing you this test, is that for what it is (you name it) it's unquestionably the world's greatest buy.

Interestingly, the writer of this report, in common with so many others, found little to criticize in the Kombi. Its lack of performance was noted but taken for granted, because no one expected a vehicle of this kind to lay rubber on the tarmac. With just 25bhp, high performance was out of the question.

THE RANGE-TOPPING *SONDERMODELL*

With some 8,500 Panelvans and people carriers sold during 1950, further increases in sales of these models in 1951, and a healthy outlook for the Beetle, Volkswagen began to make good profits. These were ploughed directly back into the company and invested in future projects. The German economy was recovering well from the devastation of the past, and the country was beginning to enjoy a certain 'feelgood factor'. By April 1951, the people at Wolfsburg were ready to launch what would quickly become the most desirable and sought-after of the classic Split-Screen Buses.

Popularly known as the 'Samba', the *Sondermodell* ('special model'), or Microbus De Luxe, was designed to broaden the appeal of the Transporter range, and to reflect the dawning of a new age.

Exterior

The Samba differed from the Kombi and standard Microbus in a number of details; its interior was brighter, lighter and more luxurious, with a more airy ambience. This was achieved principally by increasing the glass area. Behind the cab doors, along the sides of the body, were four square windows, instead of three rectangular ones, and a wrap-around window at each of the rear quarters. Four skylights were fitted on each side of the roof panel, and a Golde sunroof – an extra-cost option on the other models – came as standard.

In keeping with contemporary trends, the two-tone paintwork was embellished with bright trim. The Samba was the only model to have chromed hubcaps and a similarly plated VW roundel on the front panel. In addition, there were chunky, polished alloy mouldings fitted on top of the Y-shaped swage lines on the nose, which ran along the cab doors, and along the sides of the bodywork just below the windows. There was a further alloy moulding attached to the outside of each sill, or rocker panel.

Interior

The interior was similarly luxurious, with piped and fluted upholstery in both the cab and passenger cells, a full headlining, and carpeting on the floor of the rear luggage compartment. There were also chromed rails in this area for securing suitcases and bags, a number of coat hooks, and a large ashtray secured to the wall behind the cab seats.

To ease entry to the rear seats, the backrest of the seat nearest to the side doors was split, and folded forward. This modern touch put the Samba years ahead of its time, in terms of design thinking.

The cab differed from that of the other models. Until March 1955, the Samba was the only member of the range that had a 'full width' dashboard. Similar in design to the dashboard of the split-window Beetle, this metal panel was painted in body colour and, in addition to the speedometer, there was a large mechanical clock in front of the passengers. A blanking plate sat in the centre of the dashboard, and this could be removed for the purpose of fitting a radio, which was almost always a German Blaupunkt.

Also in contrast to the other models, the Samba's three-spoke steering wheel, switch-gear and gear-lever knob were usually coloured in cream rather than black, and this contributed to the lighter and more glamorous feel of the interior.

With seating for up to nine, the Samba was the Ritz of the range; although it was comparatively expensive to buy, there was never a shortage of customers for this range-topper. Although the Kombi outsold it many times over, sales of the de luxe Microbus continued to rise steadily right up until the end of Split-Screen production, in 1967.

A TRUCK OF ALL TRADES: THE PICK-UP

A pick-up truck would have been an inevitable and commonsense addition to the range from its inception, but a lack of finance and time delayed its public debut until August 1952. Production required a major re-think by the design team, and an expensive re-tooling exercise, because the Pick-Up, as its appearance suggests, was considerably more than a 'cut-and-shut' Panelvan.

Apart from the much smaller roof panel, the cab remained the same in construction as that of the Panelvan, as did the fixtures and fittings, but a series of new panels was devised for the new truck body. The bed needed to be flat, and this necessitated the re-siting and re-designing of the fuel tank. It was made much flatter, and repositioned above and to the right of the gearbox, with the fuel filler neck on the right-hand side of the body-work. At this stage, the other models retained the large, bulky fuel tank on the left-hand side, high up in the engine compartment.

The Pick-Up's spare wheel could not be accommodated in its more usual horizontal position above the engine, and it was there-fore moved to a specially formed well behind the driver's seat. From August 1962, it found its final resting place, in the locker bed below the bed. Air-cooling louvres for the engine were cut into the body behind the rear wheel arches.

With a steel bed of 45sq ft and a further 20sq ft of space in the weather-tight locker bed, accessed through a top-hinged door on the right-hand side of the body, the Pick-Up became a firm favourite among traders all over the world. Workers in building and construction, plumbing, gardening and land-scaping took quickly to this Volkswagen.

The two hinged side flaps and tailgate, when in the down position, gave a convenient loading and unloading height to the bed, and the bed itself was fitted with fifteen strips of hardwood. These not only strengthened the panel beneath them, but also helped to prevent the load from slipping. A canvas tarpaulin that fitted easily over a series of steel bows was offered as an extra-cost option and, with this in place, the truck boasted a useful 161cu ft of load space, with the cargo well protected from the elements.

As with the Panelvan, specialist coach-builders had a field day with the Pick-Up, as more and more uses were found for the vehicle. By the mid-1960s, there was a custom body for virtually every purpose, including special glass-carrying racks, steel cages to house livestock, steel boxes grafted on to the bed for the sales and service industries, turntables and ladders for the German fire service, jinkers and trailers for the forestry industry, and a whole host of other weird and wonderful designs.

Pick-ups sold almost as well as Panelvans, a peak of 39,458 units being reached in 1963, but, as they tended to lead such a hard life, relatively few survive today. They are now held in such high esteem that enthusiasts will go to almost any lengths to restore Split-Screen trucks, especially those comparatively crude examples that were built before March 1955, when sweeping changes were made across the entire range.

THE SIX-SEATER DOUBLE-CAB

Spreading the Load

In October 1958, the Pick-Up was optionally available with a wooden platform or as a wide-bed, with an extended bed at the sides that overhung the lower bodywork. These two variants were largely made in response to demands from the building trade for extra carrying capacity.

A month later, in November, Volkswagen launched another variation on the highly successful theme in the form of the six-seater double-cab, or crew-cab, Pick-Up. Although this workhorse was principally aimed at trades people, and more particularly the building and construction industry, it was quickly recognized as a dual-purpose family vehicle. It became extremely popular in America, almost as a fashion accessory.

The cab extension required expensive new tooling at the factory; a larger roof panel was needed, there were new body panels, a rear cab-side door, a shorter bed and revised cab.

The enlarged cab also led to the loss of the single-cab Pick-Up's locker bed, but a small number of tools and equipment of modest proportions could be stored in the space below the rear bench seat. This vehicle suited small gangs of builders, plumbers, plasterers and carpenters down to the ground. There was ample room for sand, cement and timber on the bed, which, incidentally, still came with fifteen strips of hardwood, to protect the metalwork and prevent the load slipping.

And the double-cab model scored over the single-cab in offering more accommodation for folk travelling to and from work.

RESPONSE OF THE PRESS

In some quarters, the double-cab was misunderstood. In North America, where the leisure opportunities for a vehicle of this kind were spotted almost immediately, it was criticized by journalists. This was rather unfair, since Volkswagen had never intended it as anything other than an addition to the utility Pick-Up range. One problem with the Pick-Up was that, from a driver's point of view, it was similar to a saloon car – it handled well, gave reasonable fuel consumption and its build quality was peerless in the world of mass production – and some journalists began to compare it with a car. It was most unlike any other pick-up truck.

The extent to which the double-cab was misunderstood is illustrated by *Motor Life*'s road test in the March 1960 issue. On the one hand, the writer of the report commented that:

> Volkswagen's six-passenger transporter is truly an all-round vehicle. It is a versatile

In place of the turning T-handle, the engine lid was lockable with a large key from March 1955. The same key was used for the Pick-Up's locker bed.

workhorse, an adequate sedan and can provide excellent transportation for nearly any kind of outdoor vacation. The VW handles well, has superior economy and is remarkably well constructed. The transporter's overall design combines the best features of a pick-up and a sedan into a vehicle that is successful in total design and in nearly all minor details.

These compliments reflected accurately the views of most owners but, on the other hand, the report went on:

Entry into the passenger compartment is not good by any standards. The VW sits high and requires a long step from the ground to the floorboards. Driver and passengers sit in a straight-back position and on long trips this promotes comfort although it seems unnatural at first. Both front and rear seats lack depth, legroom is adequate and headroom generous.

In common with so many others, this journalist, while appreciating the vehicle's positive attributes, had missed the point. A small child might well have experienced difficulties climbing into the cab, but Volkswagen's engineering staff had designed the cab more with a gang of bricklayers in mind.

After the Samba, the double-cab Pick-Up is arguably the most sought-after of the Split-Screen range, particularly among young enthusiasts, and it is not difficult to understand why. With sufficient space to carry people and a large quantity of luggage, its design is still relevant today in an age when multi-purpose vehicles are taking an increasing share of the automotive market.

THE HIGH-ROOF PANELVAN

For the 1962 model year, Volkswagen launched the final addition to the range – the high-roof, or high-top, Panelvan. With

Post-1955 Buses had smaller wheels – down from 16in to 15in – which helped to reduce unsprung weight.

its enlarged steel roof, taller doors and extended body panels, this model measured 90in (228.5cm) from the ground to the top of the roof, compared with the standard Panelvan's 75¾in (192.5cm).

The additional space broadened the Transporter's appeal even further and, again, there was no shortage of customers. The German Post Office, and members of the clothing and glazing trades all appreciated the additional height and load-carrying capacity. In private hands, many of these vehicles (as well as the regular Panelvans) were converted into campers, the additional headroom proving a real bonus when it came to activities like cooking. Not long after its launch, private catering firms also began to see the potential of the high-roof for a mobile café; fitted with deep-pan fryers and gas-fired cookers, the high-roof Panelvan became a popular refreshment post in the lay-bys of mainland Europe and North America. Among other enterprising adaptors were companies who turned these vehicles into mobile hairdressing salons.

IMPROVEMENTS TO THE SPLITTIE RANGE

Nordhoff's Austerity

The early Buses were a breath of fresh air at the time, but, with the wisdom of hindsight, it is fair to say that they were much too austere in almost every respect. However, they were markedly improved through the years. The Bus was probably subjected to more production improvements than any other commercial, although in essence it remained unchanged. Volkswagen's engineers, some of Europe's best, never stopped looking for ways to improve the vehicle, even if those working in the dealer network occasionally had great problems in under-

---

A tough life

Because transporters had proved capable of withstanding heavy tasks – even ploughing and harrowing – the legendary reputation for ruggedness and reliability was well established by the end of the 1950s. Generally, it would carry on for thousands of miles long after it was due for routine servicing, and there was an army of dealers equipped with spare parts if it did not.

In 1957, the *Eastern Daily Press* wrote about Austrian Franz Schartner, who used his Kombi as a taxi to transport skiers to the top of the Grossglockner Pass. His regular run – a round trip of 150 miles (240km) – to the summit of the 8,430ft (2,530m) mountain, with eight passengers and all their ski equipment aboard, was accomplished mostly in second gear. After the first 62,000 miles (99,000km), the Bus had received a 'top-end' overhaul and new brake linings. Despite such harsh punishment, Schartner recorded an average daily fuel mileage of 29–30mpg (9.43–9.75l/100km). His experience, however, was far from unique. The Volkswagen Transporter would eventually colonize almost every country in the world, including the most remote.

---

standing some of the changes. By the end of its production, the Splittie had become a reasonably refined vehicle.

Because the Bus shared so many of its mechanical components with the Beetle, changes to the specification of each model usually, but not always, took place at the same time. For a number of reasons, it is often difficult to be sure when modifications took place. Volkswagen's official records are comprehensive and detailed, but contradictory and incomprehensible in some instances; to add to the confusion, there is compelling evidence from owners that contradicts the official information. One thing is certain: the scale of the Volkswagen operation inevitably led to errors in record-keeping. Without the benefit of modern technology, administrators made mistakes, and some were so serious that they are the basis for discussion and debate among students of Volkswagen lore today.

It is also difficult to understand why some modifications took so long to go into production. For example, the tuning company Okrasa (now Oettinger) were offering twin-port cylinder heads and dual carburettors to improve the performance and 'breathing' qualities of the venerable flat-four from the early 1950s. These tuning kits worked well and demonstrated their value in rally- and race-prepared Beetles time and again, including four outright wins on the East African Safari Rally. Volkswagen refused to see the advantages of any change to this feature until the early 1970s; Nordhoff argued that such 'go-faster' items would compromise reliability. He was wrong; some engineers realized this, but it would have taken a brave man to stand up to the autocrat who paid their wages.

Throughout the 1950s, the Transporter, like the Beetle, had a petrol tank with a reserve of one gallon (4.5 litres), the reserve being operated by a 'flip tap' in the footwell. With no means of knowing how low the fuel was, drivers often experienced the engine cutting out as a result of fuel starvation before the reserve supply could be called into use. It was embarrassing and inconvenient, and potentially dangerous, but Volkswagen did not fit a fuel gauge for a full ten years after Bus production started.

The reason behind this irrational attitude can be found in the personality of Heinz Nordhoff. As well as believing that he could not be wrong, Nordhoff had a modest and austere lifestyle. He lived in a modest house, ate frugally, drank very little and worked stoically. He disapproved strongly of 'glitz', believing that anything that was not strictly necessary

to sustain human life was a luxury and, therefore, decadent. His views changed little through the years, and were carried over into his business life; he would only consent to improvements being made when there was sufficient money in the bank to invest in them. The sales figures proved that his attitude was, by and large, correct.

Gearbox Changes

The Porsche-designed non-synchromesh gearbox that had given such sterling service in the Beetle since 1946 was automatically slotted into the Transporter in 1950. Those who had mastered the art of double-declutching and silent changing considered it to be without rival. Those who had not, did not. In response, Volkswagen modified the gearbox to include synchromesh on second, third and fourth gears. This was in 1953 and was one of the first major modifications.

Power Struggle

The 1131cc engine had proved beyond doubt that it was one of the most durable and reliable power units in mass production. With maximum power of 25bhp, however, it struggled to propel the Bus, especially after owners discovered that their vehicles would actually carry considerably more than the advised maximum payload of three quarters of a ton.

From December 1953, the entire range was fitted with a new 30bhp power unit. The unit was built to the same design as the outgoing '25-brake', but an additional five horses had been found by increasing the capacity to 1192cc (72.74cu in). This was achieved by widening the bore from 75mm to 77mm. In addition, the compression ratio was raised to 6.6:1, and the diameter of the valves was increased from 28.6mm to 30mm.

With this modest gain in power, the Bus felt more lively and the top speed rose from

50mph to 60mph (from 80km/h to 96km/h). Volkswagen thoughtfully placed a sticker on the dashboard, warning owners not to exceed 50mph; it is likely that few took notice of it.

Road & Track's December 1956 road test figures revealed that the new Bus would do 16mph (25km/h) in bottom gear, 20mph (32km/h) in second and 45mph (72km/h) in third, with the benchmark figure of 60mph (96km/h) being achieved from rest in a staggeringly unimpressive 75 seconds. They were not the kind of figures this esteemed sporting journal was used to publishing, but the writer of the report explained:

> Road testing a commercial vehicle may seem more than a little out of R&T's normal province, but the popularity of Volkswagen's compact, utilitarian four wheelers has risen in this country [America] where we felt an accurate record of their performance abilities would make an interesting report.

If nothing else, this demonstrates the impact the Bus had made in America. *Road & Track*'s 'normal province' was fire-breathing sports cars from Maserati, Ferrari and Porsche, but here, in the mid 1950s, they had carried out a 'performance' road test on the 30bhp Volkswagen Transporter!

With the arrival of the 30bhp engine, the lovely old-fashioned speedometer, with the needle that appeared to run backwards, was dropped in favour of a more modern and conventional style of instrument. Like the outgoing gauge, the new one was made by VDO, and had gear speed limit markings on the dial. Maximum revs in each gear were equivalent to 10mph (16km/h) in bottom, 20mph (32km/h) in second, 34mph (54.5km/h) in third and 48mph (77km/h) in top. Again, few owners took notice of these advisory limits. Volkswagen did not expect them to, and had taken the 'brave' step of calibrating the new speedometer to 70mph (110km/h).

Throughout 1954, very few changes took place, because the engineers were gearing themselves up for the 'new-look' Transporter destined for debut in March 1955. There was the move to Hanover in 1956 to be considered as well. The tail-lamps were changed from flat lenses in 1954 to the convex 'bubble' type but, in all other respects, the Bus range remained unaltered.

MARCH 1955: PEAK PROGRESS

The Transporters made during the first five years of production served their purpose particularly well, but were undoubtedly the result of 1940s design thinking. Slowly, times were changing, and even ordinary folk were beginning to demand more from their motoring. Volkswagen needed to keep abreast of things. The 'fins-and-whistles' styling of Detroit, with acres of chromium-plating, was beginning to have an influence on European designers. The people in the Wolfsburg drawing office were not about to make the Bus resemble a Buick, but the seeds of change had been sown.

Appearance

Buses made from March 1955 had a prettier frontal appearance, because of one minor modification: the front of the roof panel was extended to form a peak along the top of the windscreen. This was not just a styling exercise, but the result of a practical attempt to improve cab fresh-air ventilation. A vent covered with metal gauze was cut into the peak above the windscreen division, to allow cold air into a collection and distribution box attached to the underside of the roof panel in the cab. The rate of airflow could be controlled manually with a metal handle on the left-hand side of the box.

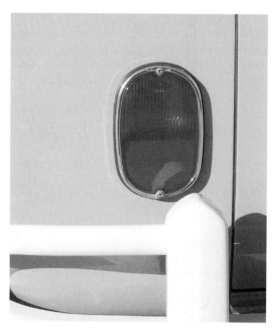

From 1958, the single brake light in the centre of the vehicle was dropped in favour of a more modern unit in each of the tail-lamp clusters.

Indicators

In response to increasing traffic, vehicles exported to North America after March 1955 were without semaphore indicators. In their place was a pair of bullet-type flashers mounted above the headlamps. The same units were fitted to European-spec vehicles from August 1961, with amber lenses rather than the clear units favoured by the Americans.

Because of the shape of the lenses, they were considered to present a potential danger to pedestrians so, from August 1961, American-spec Buses had circular and much flatter lenses. Their European counterparts followed suit two years later.

Interior

Inside the vehicle, the full-width dashboard of the de luxe Microbus was redesigned, and became a feature of the entire range. A steel parcel tray was positioned below it. Although considerably less elegant than previously, the new dashboard was more functional and modern. The single instrument – the VDO speedometer – was placed in a revised binnacle and, for the first time, incorporated all the various warning lights.

An ashtray was placed on top of the dashboard, the lid painted in body colour on all models, except on the de luxe Microbus, where it had a chromed lid. Across the range, the magnificent three-spoked steering wheel was replaced by a plastic two-spoker with the horn button at its centre. A Wolfsburg Castle emblem appeared on the boss of the Microbus de luxe, another of many small details that distinguished the top-of-the-range people carrier from the 'lesser' models. The same model also had a neat rectangular clock on the passenger's side of the dashboard, but this was much smaller than the round dial that had previously occupied this space.

Almost by accident, Volkswagen had created another practical classic. The friendly smiling 'face' had acquired something like a cloth cap on its 'head', giving the Bus the appearance of a supportive uncle.

At the rear of the Bus (except, of course, on the Pick-Up), the famous 'barn-door' engine lid was replaced by a much smaller lid at the bottom, and an opening top-hinged tailgate above it. Although this important change slightly restricted access to the engine compartment for servicing and maintenance purposes, the opening tailgate put the rear luggage area within instant reach.

At the same time, the old fashioned turning T-handle used for opening the 'barn door' was replaced by a locking mechanism operated by a large key. On Pick-Ups, this mechanism was also used for the door to the locker bed.

Because of the major bodywork changes to the rear, the spare wheel, which had previously been positioned horizontally in a narrow compartment above the engine, was re-located in the cab. This necessitated alterations to the sheet metal both below and behind the passengers' seat, resulting in the wheel being tilted at an angle in a well stamped into the cab's rear wall. This was a reasonable compromise – a similar arrangement to that of the Pick-Up – but one drawback was that, in the event of a puncture, the seat had to be removed to gain access to the wheel, and passengers would find themselves standing out in the cold.

One small modification, to improve driver comfort and convenience, was a change from a rather oddly shaped throttle pedal to

As a small concession to safety, Microbuses had softly padded, vinyl-covered sun visors from 1958.

a more conventional one covered with a thin rubber pad. Interestingly, the Beetle continued with a roller-ball throttle pedal for another two years, until it, too, got a conventional pedal.

Suspension and Wheels

In traditional German fashion, the suspension fitted to all early Buses was on the hard side of firm. However, as the roads in Europe began to get better, Volkswagen recognized the need for improving ride comfort, and duly reduced the diameter of the torsion bars from 30mm to 29mm. It was a very small change, but Volkswagen had always erred on the side of caution, and had never completely thrown tradition out of the window.

At the same time, the road wheels were reduced in diameter from 16in to 15in, with a corresponding change from 5.50 × 16 to 6.40 × 15 cross-ply tyres. Continental were the principal supplier of tyres at this time, although Michelins were favoured in some markets.

One Further Change

Later in the year, in August, there was one further change, for which all Bus owners were eternally grateful; the large 36mm nut that secured the dynamo pulley wheel was reduced in diameter to 21mm. This allowed the general-purpose spanner provided in the toolkit to be used for the sparking plugs, wheel nuts and crankshaft pulley wheel; (it was occasionally necessary to remove the latter for the purpose of changing the fan belt).

All these modifications led to a significantly different Bus – a fundamentally more modern vehicle – which, for a while, would have to suffice. The move to the Hanover plant beckoned – the first vehicles were rolling off

Compulsory in the US from 1958, the heavy American-spec bumpers became popular extra-cost options in other markets.

the assembly lines by March 1956 – and there was little time for further improvements.

FINE TUNING

Between March 1955 and May 1959, the Transporter range was, by and large, left alone. The launch of the wide-bodied Pick-Up and double-cab model kept the people in the drawing offices busy, but the vast majority of production modifications were few and far between, and went largely unnoticed.

The brake pipes were galvanized from January 1957, in one of the few rust-inhibiting measures taken by Volkswagen during the 1950s. A magnetic drain plug was fitted to the base of the gearbox as standard from March of the same year.

In May 1958, the single brake light, housed in a centrally mounted pod on the engine lid, clearly inadequate from a safety point of view, was dropped in favour of a single lamp in each of the rear light clusters. All European-spec Buses got bigger and stronger bumpers from August. At the same time, both versions of the Microbus got padded, vinyl-covered sun visors above the windscreen in place of the crude fibreboard items; this move coincided with a similar change on the Beetle.

A month later, big, heavy US-spec bumpers were introduced. These had much taller overriders, with a substantial bar passing through them, to give extra bodywork protection in increasingly restricted parking spaces on the street of North American cities and towns. Although heavier and larger many regarded these items as

Outwardly indistinguishable from the original 25bhp engine, the 30bhp unit was completely redesigned in May 1959.

aesthetic improvements; they were offered as extra-cost options in most other markets, and are now highly sought after by restorers and collectors.

By the end of the 1950s, Volkswagen had three major products – the Bus, Beetle and Karmann Ghia – that were selling beyond all expectations around the globe. Sceptics on Volkswagen's board became increasingly fearful, however, that all three vehicles would soon run their course, and customers would look elsewhere for something bigger, better and more powerful. It had, after all, been fifteen years since Beetle production had begun, and ten years since the first Transporters, and Volkswagen's rivals had launched several new and replacement models during this profitable period.

As far as Nordhoff was concerned, other manufacturers could do what they liked. He was adamant that the basic philosophy behind the Bus was correct, and stuck rigidly to his guns. His obstinacy conceded just one point – the flat-four engine was desperately in need of more power.

A NEW ENGINE DESIGN

Engine

Although to the same configuration, the new engine, introduced in May 1959, was to a wholly fresh design. Very few parts were interchangeable between the old and new, although, at first glance, they differed little in appearance.

The new unit was rated at 30bhp – the same as the outgoing unit – but it was more efficient. Improvements included much stronger crankcase halves, with stronger retaining studs and bolts to hold them together, wider spacing of the cylinders to improve engine cooling, and a sturdier crankshaft. The crankshaft it replaced was prone to breaking on high-mileage engines that were constantly driven with high revs on board. There was also a revised fuel pump drive and a detachable dynamo pedestal. The latter had previously been cast as an integral part of the right-hand half of the crankcase, and made removal of the dynamo and its associated electrical cables something of a gymnastic exercise. Removing the new pedestal – still made of alloy – was a simple matter of undoing four bolts.

Separate cam-followers were employed for the first time, and the cylinder heads were redesigned with a new shape to the combustion chambers, which had the beneficial effect of raising the compression ratio from 6.1:1 to 6.6:1. The valves were inclined at a slant and, thanks to a larger dynamo pulley wheel and a smaller crankshaft pulley wheel, the speed of the cooling fan was reduced in relation to engine revolutions. This change had the small advantage of reducing engine noise, at least from the outside.

Many wondered why Volkswagen had gone to the considerable trouble and expense of designing a new engine that produced no more power than the previous unit. After all, customers had been calling for an increase in power. The explanation was that this was an interim engine, and that there was more to come shortly.

At first the new engine also developed 30bhp, but 34bhp was available from 1960. Note that the dynamo pedestal is now detachable.

TRANSMISSION

The gearbox that accompanied the new power unit was also to a fresh and much-improved design. Similar in layout to the box fitted to the contemporary Porsche 356, there was synchromesh on all four forward speeds (instead of the top three as previously), and larger bearing assemblies were used in the internal construction. The alloy casing was also radically redesigned; instead of two castings split vertically along the centreline, there was a new one-piece 'tunnel' type with easily detachable side plates.

Mechanics in the dealer network and elsewhere particularly appreciated this change, as the much larger differential side bearings allowed the axle shafts to be extracted without the need to disassemble the transaxle unit. The main pinion shaft was also designed in such a way that shim adjustments on the shaft could be made without having to strip down the pinion assembly.

This was the start of what is known today as 'production engineering', a process by which technicians are employed to discover ways of simplifying production methods, and reducing costs as a result. Volkswagen's technicians were, and still are, masters of this science.

PRACTICE MADE PERFECT

A New Carburettor

Thirteen months after the first Transporters were fitted with the new gearbox and 'interim' power unit, the compression ratio was raised yet again, this time to 7.0:1. At the same time, the trusty and long-serving Solex 28PCI carburettor was changed for the new 28 PICT, and this resulted in engine power rising from 30bhp to a maximum 34bhp

The 1960s began with American-spec vehicles being compulsorily fitted with attractive sealed-beam headlamps.

developed at 3,400rpm. In addition, the ratio of the reduction gears in the axle hubs was altered from 1.4:1 to 1.39:1.

One advantage of the new carburettor – although not everyone saw it as an advantage – was its in-built thermostatically controlled automatic choke unit. A fairly complex mechanism, the choke valve was operated by a bi-metallic spring, and vacuum-operated piston. A heater element was also incorporated into the design, and the oil bath air cleaner was modified to include an air inlet with a weighted flap valve. A pre-heating system for the carburettor had been devised, in which a flexible pipe was connected to the left-hand heater box in the exhaust system at one end, and to the air cleaner at the other.

The mixture of hot and cold air was governed by the flap valve, which in turn was controlled by engine revs. When the temperature increased to 68 degrees Fahrenheit (20 degrees centigrade) and above, the flap valve allowed the carburettor to draw nothing but cold air in from outside.

The combined result of these modifications was a much livelier Bus, with improved acceleration and much smoother running. Volkswagen cared little at this time for one indisputable fact – that the products of rival manufacturers had engines developing more than double the brake horsepower of the humble 1200cc Volkswagen unit.

Road Test

Bus sales continued to rise by approximately 10,000 units per annum, despite some reactionary customers complaining that the new automatic choke had led to an increase in fuel consumption. Test after test proved that their protestations were simply a reaction against a 'new-fangled' device over which they had no control. Volkswagen's people working in the dealer network were used to such complaints; they listened patiently, and then ignored them.

Car Life's 1961 road test praised the revised Bus for its excellent synchromesh gearbox, its top speed of 60mph (96km/h), 'which can be maintained for hours without harm', and its ability to withstand deliberate abuse. The writer also commented, 'We also liked the braking system, which seemed equal to handling even in an overloaded vehicle on downhill grades', and added,

> Perhaps one of the biggest selling points of the VW is its economy of operation. Our test car averaged just under 20mpg [14.15l/100km] during all conditions imposed, while claims by Bus owners of 24mpg [11.8l/100km] are not infrequent. Officially, we give it a range of 18–22mpg [12.86–15.7l/100km] in normal operation; what mileage you get is highly dependent upon how heavily you tread the throttle.

As the new decade progressed, the Bus continued to be modified in detail, but Volkswagen could not afford to ignore for ever the fact that, despite major revisions to the 1192cc engine, it still produced only a paltry 34bhp.

Long overdue, the fuel gauge – a circular VDO item – made an appearance for the 1961 model year.

RESPONDING TO A CHANGING WORLD

In the 1960s, the motoring world changed faster than at any time previously. As affluence grew in the West, more and more vehicles took to the roads, inevitably leading to a corresponding increase in the number of serious road accidents. Improved vehicle safety quickly became a priority for governments on both sides of the Atlantic. Daimler-Benz led the way in the fields of primary and secondary safety, particularly employing practical concepts in the 230SL sports car, launched in 1963.

Firestone, Continental, Pirelli and Michelin were all taking part in a race to develop and perfect the radial tyre, and manufacturers were beginning to fit head restraints to seats, and seat belts. Both the Bus and Beetle changed year on year, even if only an expert would be able to spot the differences between old and new models. In some quarters, Volkswagens continued to be criticized for the supposed disadvantages of swing-axle rear suspension, and a few commentators considered the rear engine position to be inherently dangerous. (Interestingly, a number of manufacturers now widely acknowledge, as a result of crash testing, that the safest place for the engine is in the tail, out of harm's way.)

Volkswagen kicked off the new decade by fitting sealed-beam headlamps to all vehicles exported to North America. This was in direct response to new legislation making these items a mandatory requirement. With their clear glass lenses, these headlamps arguably improved the Bus's frontal appearance further, its 'eyes' becoming even more human. A long-overdue VDO fuel gauge was fitted next to the speedometer for 1961; unlike the Beetle's incongruous square item, the gauge on the Bus was circular, in keeping with the speedometer.

In June 1961, the steel grab handles on the rear passenger seats in both the Kombis and Microbuses were changed for hard plastic items, and the following month a plastic grab handle was attached to the dashboard for the benefit of front passengers. The following month, the safety theme was continued when the corners of the speedometer binnacle were rounded off and, from August 1961, all models were fitted with padded, vinyl-covered sun visors that had previously only seen service on the Microbuses.

Because of the launch of the Type 3 saloon towards the end of 1961, the Bus was treated to relatively few modifications in 1962. Improving safety and comfort would continue apace almost until the end of Split-Window production in 1967, but the launch of the Type 3 saloon – originally intended as a replacement for the aged Beetle – gave the marketing men in Hanover and Wolfsburg a useful idea.

Fitted with a 42bhp 1500cc engine, the Type 3 was the company's most powerful model; it was obvious that, with suitable modification, the power could be 'shoehorned' into the Transporter, and go a long way to answering those critics who maintained (with a deal

of justification) that the Bus in its standard 1200 form was indecently underpowered.

THE 'FIFTEEN'

Increased Power

Known as the 'suitcase' engine in Volkswagen circles, the Type 3's 1500 unit differed from the 1200 fitted to the Bus and Beetle in that its cooling fan was mounted vertically on the nose of the crankshaft at the rear of the engine. Its modified cooling trays, oil dipstick and inlet manifold conspired to give a much more compact, flatter unit, hence the nickname 'suitcase'.

The cooling fan had a large alloy shroud over it, and this meant that the unit would not slot directly into the engine compartment

The large flat indicators that replaced the 'bullets' not only improved the safety of pedestrians, but enhanced the look of the Bus.

First for the American market, the Type 3 saloon's 1500 engine arrived in 1963, and gave the Transporter a reasonable turn of speed, but ...

of the Bus. Volkswagen decided, therefore, to fit the Transporter's more conventional fan and fan housing vertically on top of the engine, and re-install the conventional cooling trays and dipstick. Technically, the result was little more than a bored-out 1200; in practice, it provided the basis for the company's best-ever air-cooled power unit, combining reliability and useable power in one neat package.

The 1,493cc capacity was achieved by increasing the bore and stroke to 83 × 69mm. The compression ratio was raised to 7.5:1, and maximum power of 42bhp was produced at just 3,800rpm. To ensure that the engine remained as durable and reliable as the 1200, Volkswagen resolutely stuck to the same single-port cylinder-head design, 28 PICT carburettor, and intentionally restrictive narrow-bore inlet manifold.

An increase of 8bhp over the 1200's 34bhp appeared to be a negligible gain, but it was sufficient to raise the top speed to 65mph (105km/h), and the payload from three quarters of a ton (750kg) to one ton (1,000kg). Some argued that Volkswagen should have considered putting the engine from the 'S' version of the Type 3 saloon into the Transporter. This had high-compression domed pistons, twin carburettors and 47bhp on tap, and would have done very nicely in answering the 'performance' critics. However, it was not to be. Performance from a Volkswagen Bus? Perish the thought.

US manufacturers were beginning to pose a serious and increasing threat to Volkswagen's dominance of the small commercials market, so the 1500 Transporter made its debut in the USA, in January 1963. A couple of months later, the 'Fifteen' as it is

... the dreaded throttle governor, fitted to the carburettor, could make overtaking a tricky business.

affectionately known, became an option in all other markets, but only in the people-carrying versions. Customers of Pick-Ups and Panelvans had to wait until the following August until they too could order the more powerful engine.

The 1200 remained an option until the autumn of 1965, when it finally bowed out, but the vast majority of customers had plumped for the bigger engine from its inception. To cope with the additional power, the gear ratios were altered as follows: first 3.80:1. second 2.06:1, third 1.26:1, top 0.82:1, reverse 3.61:1, final-drive ratio 4.125:1, reduction gearboxes 1.26:1.

A Carburettor Governor

Customers drove their new Fifteens with renewed and undisguised pleasure, but, as stories about high-speed delivery vans 'racing' Porsche 356s on German roads

began to filter back to Volkswagen, the company's lawyers and advisors began to be concerned. Bus owners were coming to realize that the 1500 engine, when 'bedded in' properly, would give greater performance than its modest specification might suggest.

Volkswagen's claimed top speed of 65mph (105km/h) was clearly incorrect, and the true speed in most cases was in excess of 75mph (120km/h). Fearful of the consequences of a fully laden delivery van crashing out of control at such high speed – with writs arriving on Nordhoff's desk from injured third parties – Volkswagen took steps to restrain the driving habits of free-spirited Bus owners. From August 1964, all 1500s had a governor fitted to the carburettor.

In theory, this move was a reasonable solution to a real problem, but thousands of owners showed their displeasure by taking a spanner to their governor and removing it.

The governor led to a lack of power when overtaking and climbing steep hills, necessitating tiresome shifting down through the gearbox. In one sense, it was back to square one.

Despite this, *Hot Rod Special* commented in 1963 that 'there are very few hills that will faze the VW – even when loaded to the gunwales'. The writer was not so confident, though, about descending steep hills. He wrote:

> Brakes have always been just adequate on Volkswagens. The wagons with the 1500 engines have 159 square inches of lining area as compared to 130 square inches on the standard-engined wagon. They do a satisfactory job and it would be only in extreme conditions – fully loaded down a steep mountain grade – where significant fade might be encountered. In such an event it would be hoped that the driver would be descending in a low gear to help compensate.

By the beginning of August 1965, Volkswagen had partially addressed the problems posed by the carburettor governor. The 28 PICT Solex was replaced by the more efficient 28 PICT 1, and, more importantly, the inlet valves were increased in diameter from 31.5mm to 35.5mm, and the exhausts from 30mm to 32mm. The valve changes made a big difference to the engine's ability to 'breathe' throughout the entire rev range, even if maximum power only went up by a modest 2bhp, to 44bhp. These engines felt strong, pulled willingly and sounded magnificent – three reasons why journalists and devotees received them so well.

Increased Success

Detroit continued to produce their V8s, but the Bus reigned supreme. The quality of its build, paint finish, fixtures and fittings was clearly without rival. Some still considered the Bus to be ugly, but compared with its nearest rivals it remained stunningly beautiful. It certainly lost out against American rivals in the performance stakes, despite the increase in power, but it had a trump card to play. Fuel mileage worked out at 24–29mpg (9.75–11.79l/100km), and general running costs were roughly half those associated with other light commercial vehicles.

With the introduction of the 1500 engine, sales figures again increased worldwide. Nearly 188,000 units were sold in 1964, compared with 175,000 for the previous year. Panelvans remained the staple diet of the range, with Kombis running a close second, and the specially kitted out Ambulance bringing up the rear as usual. Camper versions also continued to gain ground, as more and more people discovered the advantages of an economical vehicle that saved on hotel bills.

By 1962, Volkswagen had produced their millionth Transporter, and had become Europe's largest vehicle manufacturer, regularly outselling nearest rivals, Fiat, Ford and BMC. Beetles were rolling off the Wolfsburg assembly lines at a rate of one every four seconds, and the Transporter continued to prove its worth in both the developed and developing world.

In 1963, *Hot Rod Special* concluded:

> In spite of a few disbelievers who can't see why anyone would actually want to ride around in one of those funny looking things, there seems no doubt that the VW wagon is here to stay. The boldly practical concept is just too good to pass by. Apparently then, the only thing between the VW and total public acceptance is the attitude of misinformed parking lot attendants. Or are they misinformed? After all, some of them are trucks, aren't they?

With the 1500 Bus, Volkswagen had pulled off another master stroke, and not before time. Had the quest (following pleas from owners) for more power been left any longer, it is difficult to imagine the Bus surviving so long, let alone retaining its place at number one on the commercials bestseller list.

DEVELOPMENT CONTINUES

Whereas the majority of the world's motor manufacturers had fallen into the well-worn groove of launching wholly new or 'facelifted' models on an annual basis, Volkswagen's Transporter remained almost (but not quite) the same as ever. Volkswagen's engineers continued to make minor changes, and these were incorporated into the design each August. Most of the modifications were trivial, but the more knowledgeable sales staff rarely missed an opportunity to bring the important ones to the attention of showroom browsers.

Apart from the introduction of the 1500 engine in 1963, one major and welcome change was made to the exhaust and heating system. Prior to 1963, the heating system had been integrated into the engine cooling system – heat produced by the engine was used for heating the passenger compartment and cab. In effect, the cooling fan blew hot air over the crankcase, cylinder barrels and cylinder heads, and some of this air was utilized by the heater boxes on the front of the exhaust, and ducted through to the vehicle's interior.

Regulation of the heating system was controlled by a knob on the floor of the cab near the driver's seat. This knob operated two heater-control valves, and the engine-heater flaps on the two heater boxes, via a cable running through the centre of the floor. When the heater knob was screwed in a clockwise direction, the heat control valve was in a closed position, and the engine-cooling air outlet flap was open. On this setting, the engine-cooling air was expelled at the rear of the vehicle. When the control knob was screwed in an anti-clockwise direction, the cool air outlet flap closed, and the heater control flap opened, with the result that warm air was directed into the cabin.

Like many designs that grew out of Professor Porsche's genius, this system was incredibly simple and worked well, but it had one major disadvantage. In time, the air-cooled engine tended to develop oil leaks, particularly from the pushrod seals. When the oil was combined with mud and other grime from the road, the cylinder heads, barrels and crankcase would inevitably become encrusted. Air blown over this filth would find its way into the cab and rear passenger area, and the smell would be unpleasant, to say the least. The only solution was to remove the engine, clean it and cure the offending oil leak, but this was a time-consuming and potentially expensive business.

The problem was solved by changing the heater boxes for heat exchangers. This new system worked on a principle similar to the old one, in that there was a valve and flap system operated by a cable-controlled knob in the cab. However, instead of hot air being blown over the engine and ducted into the interior, it was taken from large metal chambers built around the exhaust pipes.

The hot exhaust heated the air in the chambers, which, having been nowhere near the barrels, heads and crankcase, was guaranteed to be odour-free. Still used today on air-cooled engines built at Volkswagen's Puebla plant in Mexico, the heat exchanger system is theoretically foolproof. Rust in the exhaust system, however, can in old age lead to holes, which results in carbon monoxide finding its way into the heater system; this is an obvious threat to health of driver and passengers. Some years ago, one or two journalists in search of a scoop picked up on this, and sought to condemn and discredit air-cooled Volkswagens for this potential threat. In response, Porsche's experimental department took an air-cooled Volkswagen, punctured several holes in its exhaust system, and carefully measured carbon monoxide levels in the cabin. The results were interesting – the level was virtually identical to the result of a couple of people enjoying a cigarette each!

Although contemporary road testers praised both the old heater boxes and new heat exchangers for their ability to defrost the windscreen and heat the passenger areas quickly, it is a commonly held belief today that the Transporter's heating system is one of the worst to be found in a commercial vehicle. The problem stems, however, from non-original parts being fitted; although they might be considerably cheaper than genuine Volkswagen parts, they do not have the same thermo-dynamic properties.

From August 1963, small external changes began to be made. For European-spec Buses, the rear light clusters gained an amber sector at the top of each lens for the indicator function; this coincided with the same vehicles changing over to flat, circular flashers on the front panel. American-spec Transporters had a red lens at the rear for the indicator function.

Also from 1963, the engine-cooling louvres on the outside of the rear bodywork were cut to face inwards rather than outwards, as previously. At the rear, both the tailgate and window were made substantially wider. The latter improved rearward visibility, in response to increasing traffic. At the same time, the T-handle lock on the tailgate was changed for a push-button item, and the tailgate was modified to include a finger indentation beneath for ease of operation. A similar push-button mechanism was fitted to the cab doors from December 1963.

As a result of the wider tailgate glass, the wrap-around windows on the rear quarters of the de luxe Microbus – a distinct feature of this model since the start of production – were banished to the history books. The classic 23-window Samba became the 21-window Bus, a fact that would be reflected significantly in the value of the two models in years to come. The range-topping luxury Bus remained a classic among Transporters, but dropping the wrap-around windows marked something of a turning point; it was a visual reminder that the fun of carefree motoring days was beginning to give way to the increasing demands of a more modern world.

WHEELING IN THE YEARS

In August 1963, the 15in road wheels were reduced in diameter to 14in. This was a slightly odd and costly move, in view of the fact that Volkswagen's other models – the Beetle, Type 3 saloon and Karmann Ghia sports car – continued to sit on 15in wheels. The new 14in items had the advantage of reducing unsprung weight, but by an insignificant amount, which went largely unnoticed by owners.

In essence, the design of the wheels had not changed, except for the two reductions in diameter. The same five-bolt design had been used throughout production. Immensely strong and simple in construction, Transporter wheels were always supplied and fitted by the factory in a single colour – white. All models in the range had matching painted hubcaps, except the Samba, which had chromed items. Throughout the 1950s and 60s, however, dozens of Transporters had their wheels painted in a variety of colour combinations, mostly by owners and dealers. Two-tone black and white, or black and grey were popular, and many chose body colour combinations, but chromium-plating, which has found favour with several restorers today, was never a factory-supplied option.

The domed hubcaps, such a strong styling feature until 1970, when they were replaced by less shapely, flatter items, had VW emblems at their centre, painted in a variety of colours, but more usually black. After 1964, the V-over-W emblem remained as a stamping, but was not painted. Aggrieved at Volkswagen's seeming want to spoil the ship for the sake of a ha'p'orth of tar, several owners continued with the old tradition, and painted the emblems themselves.

With the change to 14in wheels, the tyres were altered in size to 7.00 × 14, supplied as before either by Continental or Michelin. In keeping with old traditions these too followed every 'tramline' and irregularity in the road surface.

TWILIGHT YEARS

Between 1964 and 1966, sales of Split-Screen Transporters remained exceptionally healthy. From a high of nearly 188,000 units in 1964 to 176,000 in 1966, there was no sharp decline until the final year, when the announcement of the new Bay-Window model resulted in the production of just 68,100 Splitties.

November 1963 had seen the oil bath air cleaner above the carburettor moved from the left-hand side of the engine bay to the

From August 1963, the road wheels were reduced in diameter again, from 15in to 14in.

Although it is difficult to appreciate the safety aspect, the engine-cooling louvres were cut to face inwards from August 1963.

right-hand side, but serious development of the design was slowly coming to an end. In May 1964, the Solex carburettor was fitted with a larger and more efficient automatic choke, and much-needed longer wind-screen-wiper blades came in the August of the same year. The following month, the headlining in both versions of the Microbus was changed from soft cloth to white vinyl. This had the effect of dramatically bright-ening up the interior, making it more airy and giving it a more modern feel. As a bonus, the vinyl material was much easier to clean.

Throughout almost all of 1965, the Bus was left well alone. Volkswagen had spent much of the previous year preparing for the launch of the substantially revised and all-new 1300-engined Beetle and, as had been

the case on so many previous occasions, development of the Transporter was put on the back burner.

In August 1965, minor improvements included a wider rear cab window for the Pick-Up, a two-speed windscreen wiper across the range (although, with the 6-volt battery to power it, few noticed the differ-ence between the two speeds), and push-button control to open the engine lid. In addition, the oil filler neck – an awkwardly positioned casting built into the dynamo pedestal – was increased in diameter, and the headlamp dipswitch was moved, from the floor next to the clutch pedal to the stalk on the left-hand side of the steering column. These were small revisions, but most own-ers thought them to be worthwhile. As for the bigger picture, there was little to get excited about.

THE ITALIAN JOB

From August 1965, Transporters exported to Italy came with the option of Volks-wagen's recently introduced 1300 engine. For the home and all other markets, this power unit was only available in the Beetle. It was an acceptably good 'halfway house' between the 1200 and 1500 units, and pro-duced a useful 40bhp at 4,000rpm. Like the 1200 and 1500, the 1300 used single-port cylinder heads and a single Solex carburet-tor, but produced power over and above that of the 1200 by utilizing the crankshaft from the 1500 Type 3 saloon. This lengthened the stroke from 64mm to 69mm, which took the overall capacity to 1,285cc. The compres-sion ratio was also raised, from 7:1 to 7.3:1, a little less than on the 1500s, but a useful gain all the same.

Not surprisingly, the versatile Trans-porter was a great success in Italy, particu-larly with Italian tradesmen, despite the existence of a similar, much smaller home-grown product from Fiat's factories in Turin.

I remember family holidays in Italy during the early 1970s, with a Volkswagen Bus flavour. Each evening, returning from the beach resort of Chiavari on the Mediterranean coast to our rented house in the hills, some twenty-five miles of testing hairpin bends away, we always stopped on the side of the road for a long picnic. It was a most pleasant way of spending an hour or so, lapping up the evening sunshine and chatting. And I clearly recall that, every evening for a whole month, the peace and tranquillity was momentarily shattered by an Italian maniac in a green single-cab Pick-Up. His companion would be swigging from a large bottle of red wine, in between huge puffs on a cigarette, while the driver

himself hurled the old Bus, which had seen better days, around the bends as if he were Lauda in a Grand Prix Ferrari. The broken exhaust pipe made an extraordinarily loud noise, which echoed off the rocks on the sides of the roads for mile after mile. All that was needed to complete the picture was a commentary from Murray Walker!

LIGHTING-UP TIME

During the last year of Splittie production, Volkswagen made one of the most useful modifications, which almost superseded in importance all the others put together. From August 1966, the switch was made from 6- to 12-volt electrics, a year before the Beetle was treated to the same luxury.

For the 1964 model year, the rear window was made considerably wider, to improve visibility.

A direct consequence of the larger rear window, the Samba lost its wrap-around windows and became known as the '21-Window' Bus.

The 12-volt system had been an extra-cost option during the final four years of the Split-Screen's production life, but it was an expensive one for which few customers were prepared to pay. Generally, the 6-volt system had given reasonably good service and, because most of the components in this electrical system were so much smaller than those in the 12-volt system, 6-volt Buses were a little lighter overall.

Against this small advantage, though, were two irritating drawbacks; the headlamps were totally inadequate, as were the tail-lamps and brake lights, and the battery was notorious for suffering from voltage drop in cold weather. In the depths of a particularly cold winter, Bus owners living in Britain, Canada and the colder parts of mainland Europe became thoroughly disenchanted with Herr Bosch's little batteries.

The change to 12-volt electrics was a welcome one.

The new 12-volt Bosch battery continued to be housed on the right-hand side of the engine compartment but, being bigger, it took up a little more space. All the electrical components were up-rated to cope with the extra power; most significantly, the starter motor was increased in output from 0.5bhp to 0.7bhp, and the flywheel ring gear had its teeth increased in number, from 109 to 130.

The benefits of these changes were many; provided the electrical system was kept in good order, the engine would never fail to start, even in the coldest atmospheric conditions, and the lighting system did the job for which it was designed. With 45/40-watt headlamp bulbs, the road ahead was still dimly lit, but night driving was no longer the slow, frustrating experience it had been with the 6-volters. A number of Transporters were converted to 12 volts by dealers and owners retrospectively, and this trend continues among restorers today.

SPLIT ENDS

During the last few years of Splittie production, journalists continued to write about these vehicles – particularly the Camper versions – with the kind of enthusiasm more normally associated with Ferraris and other exotica. Contemporary road testers found it virtually impossible to find fault with the Bus, at a time when vitriol had been aimed at so many other vehicles.

In 1966, the American editor of *Foreign Car Guide* wrote the following about a camping-equipped de luxe Microbus:

As with all the Kombi family, it was no speed demon, but it would cruise easily at about 55mph [88km/h], and on a gradient would hold 50mph [80km/h] if you pushed the accelerator to the floor and held it there. Getting started was also a matter of flooring it and building up the revs in each gear so you could hit the torque peak for the upshift. But then this vehicle has a truck in its ancestry, and it was designed to handle heavy loads. Perhaps it was not meant to handle loads this heavy, but it can and does completely. A sports car it is not, but a useful vehicle it most certainly is.

In its final year of production, the Splittie gained 12-volt electrics, was powered by Volkswagen's best air-cooled engine – the 1500 – and was a civilized daily driver. The world had, however, changed and the first-generation Bus was at the end of its development.

In Britain, *Motor* magazine tested the Danbury Multicar – a camping version of the Kombi – as late as May 1967, and, although the launch of the Bay-Window was just a few months away, praise and admiration for the ageing Splittie kept coming. The writer of *Motor*'s report enjoyed the comfortable driving position, easy-to-operate pedals, powerful fade-free brakes, and ability to stop and restart on a 1-in-3 uphill incline. He also commented,

> The most endearing thing is its ability to cruise at near its top speed without undue mechanical noise. Even passengers in the body of the van are no more conscious of the rear-mounted engine than the driver. Add to this a low level of wind noise at speed and the result is the ability to achieve quite high average speeds without tiring the passengers.

He continued in much the same vein about the precise handling, the suspension's ability to deal with every type of road surface – 'a vehicle that gives complete confidence to the driver' – rattle-free bodywork, and a surprisingly good fuel consumption figure of 29.2mpg (9.69l/100km). In fact, there was no criticism of any kind in his report.

Practical, fun, and already with a global cult following, the last of the Split-Screen Transporters were really quite special. With such a comprehensive range, there was a model that catered for everyone's needs.

The cult of the Transporter was acknowledged in Tom Robbins' best-selling novel, *Even Cowgirls Get The Blues*:

> From the supposed direction of the ranch there approached a VW Microbus. It was painted with mandalas, lamaistic dorjes and symbols representing 'the clear light of the void' – quite an adornment for the vehicular flower of German industry.

Despite many changes down the years, the Splittie had always retained its essential character. By July 1967, that character had endeared itself to 1.8 million largely happy customers. In itself, there was little that could be faulted in the vehicle, but it was 'pensioned off' at the right time – while it was still on top. Competition from other manufacturers – who had all copied Volkswagen's original concept – was growing stronger every year, and Volkswagen could not ignore the financial perils of carrying on with what was becoming an out-of-date product.

Although many owners were undoubtedly devoted to their Splitties – many dyed-in-the-wool aficionados vowed that they would never drive anything else – the replacement model launched in August 1967 was clearly superior in almost every way. Sales figures clearly support Volkswagen's timely decision to modernize the Bus. For many, though, the Split-Screen would always remain the classic among the world's people and goods carriers.

3 Bay-Window Buses: The Second Generation

The mid-1960s was a frantically busy time for Volkswagen's design team, and an exciting one for the German giant's increasingly loyal clientele. In August 1966, the company debuted the new 1500 Beetle, a fabulous car even by Volkswagen's incomparable standards. At the same time, preparations were well under way for the launch of the new Type 4 saloon – another model that was ultimately intended as a replacement for the Beetle –

but it was the unveiling of the new Transporter that made the biggest impact on those who closely followed Volkswagen's fortunes.

A MODERN NEW DESIGN

Bigger, bolder and modern in every respect, the second-generation Bay-Window Bus was to a wholly new design. Unlike the

Bigger and more modern in every way, the Bay-Window model was launched in August 1967. The range was complete from the beginning and, despite bland styling, sales rose inexorably.

Volkswagen Transporter 1967–79

Specification

Body type   Unitary construction

Engine

Type	Air-cooled horizontally opposed 4-cylinder
Capacity	1584cc
Bore	85.5mm
Stroke	69.0mm
Compression ratio	7.5:1
Cylinders	Detachable cast-iron barrels
Cylinder heads	Made of light alloy with two valves per cylinder, operated by a single camshaft and pushrods
Fuel system	Single Solex carburettor
Maximum power	50bhp
Maximum torque	74.5lb/ft at 2,800rpm

Gears

Gearbox	Baulk synchronized 4-speed manual with hypoid bevel gear final drive in common alloy housing
Gear ratios	First 3.80:1, second 2.06:1, third 1.26:1, fourth 0.89:1, reverse 3.61:1, final drive 4.125:1
Clutch	Single dry-plate

Suspension, brakes and steering

Front suspension	Transverse torsion bars with parallel trailing arms, telescopic shock absorbers and anti-roll bar
Rear suspension	Transverse torsion bars, trailing arms and telescopic shock absorbers
Brakes	Dual circuit, hydraulically operated drums; front discs from 1970 on all models
Steering	Worm and roller
Wheels and tyres	Pressed steel 5-bolt 5.5J × 14 with 7.00 × 14 8PR cross-plies or 185R 14C radials depending on model

Dimensions

Overall length	174.6in (443.5cm)
Overall width	66.6in (169.25cm)
Overall height	76in (193cm)
Wheelbase	93in (236.25cm)
Front track	54in (137.25cm)
Rear track	56.6in (143.75cm)
Ground clearance	7.9in (19.75cm)
Fuel tank capacity	13.2 gallons (59.93 litres)
Unladen weight	5,070lb (2,305kg)

Performance

Maximum speed	68mph (109km/h)
0–50mph (0–80km/h)	23secs
Standing quarter mile	26.5secs
Fuel consumption	24.8mpg (11.4l/1100km) (official Volkswagen figure)

(For the specification for the later 1700, 1800 and 2-litre models, *see* text.)

Split-screen range, the Bay-Window range – Kombi, Microbus, Microbus De Luxe, Panelvan, high-roof Panelvan, single- and double-cab Pick-Ups – was available right from the beginning of production. At the same time, the 1300 and 1500 Beetles were 'facelifted' and modernized to comply with

Heinz Nordhoff's policy of constant reinvestment of profits paid handsome dividends. By the time of his death in 1968, Volkswagen was Europe's leading motor manufacturer.

the demands of American legislation; the new cars shared many components with the new Transporter range.

Aesthetically, the Bay was not as happy as the vehicle it replaced. The frontal appearance was no longer that of a smiling human face. The Y-shaped swage lines on the front panel, the split windscreen and the pretty peak over the top of the windscreen, all of which had contributed so much to the appealing character of the Splittie, had disappeared.

What Volkswagen decreed was right for the new world was a rather bland, yet totally functional vehicle, with a 'no-nonsense' approach. Journalists who tested early examples were not brave enough to use the word 'ugly' to describe the new Bus, but they certainly hinted that Volkswagen's styling department might have put a little more thought into cheering up the design. Wisely, contemporary commentators left it to members of the car-buying public to decide whether they liked the styling or not. Fortunately for Volkswagen, they did.

As it turned out, the Bay's aesthetics were relatively unimportant, because the vehicle's strongest points lay elsewhere. The American publication *Popular Imported Cars* commented in March 1968,

While safety and smog occupy much of the 1968 automotive headline news, appearance, comfort, convenience, handling, ride and utility are additional nouns you can use to describe the new Volkswagen 'boxes', the Beetle's harder working cousin.

SOLID FOUNDATIONS

Exterior

Five inches (12.5cm) longer than the vehicle it replaced, and with a 27 per cent larger, one-piece 'wrap-around' windscreen, the Bay was built on the same principle as the Splittie. There was a sturdy chassis frame with two main longitudinals braced with crossmembers, and outriggers to support the sills and outer bodywork. The longitudinals ran the entire length of the vehicle, rising only where they needed to clear the front and rear suspension units. As before, the frame was welded and integrated into the underbody; in effect, this made for a unitary construction body/chassis unit. Regrettably, Volkswagen, in common with the majority of manufacturers at the time, took few steps to protect the chassis from corrosion. Dealers applied underseal if requested, but this had a tendency to dry out, crack and retain rainwater, with inevitable consequences.

Changes to the body were obvious and instantly recognizable. The front panel was changed to give a flatter appearance, and had rectangular indicators located below the headlamps. A fresh air grille – a most up-to-date feature – sat above them, and a large VW roundel was positioned in the centre of the panel.

On people-carrying Buses, there were three long rectangular windows on either side of the vehicle (instead of the Splittie's four square ones), which gave a modern and much sleeker appearance. Except on the Pick-Up, the air-intake louvres for ducting cool air to the engine were placed high up on the side panels, behind the rear side windows. This move helped to prevent excessive quantities of dust from the road getting into the engine compartment, and was one of many real improvements.

The Bay's frontal appearance was still reminiscent of a human face, but it seemed less inclined to 'smile' than the Splittie – a reflection, perhaps, on changing attitudes of the day.

The cab doors were some 2½in (6.25cm) wider, giving easier access to the cab, but the most striking and useful of all the body changes was a sliding door on the side of the body. This also improved access, but its biggest advantage was appreciated by commercial operators, who could make 'pavement' deliveries without the doors obstructing pedestrians. As before, this door was located on the opposite side to the driver (whether left- or right-hand drive), and operated by a large, typically 'hewn-from-the-solid' turning handle.

An opening quarter light was fitted to the cab doors; on passenger-carrying Buses, a second in the left rear side window and a third opposite the sliding door were available as extra-cost options. With safety very much a central theme of the design, two much larger rectangular rear-view mirrors were bolted to the outside of both cab doors, and the interior rear-view mirror was similarly enlarged.

Reflecting increasing traffic problems, particularly in urban areas, the front and rear bumpers were made bigger, squarer and stronger, and wrapped around all four corners. At the front they were flattened on their ends and fitted with a rubber cover to provide a step up into the cab.

Unlike on the Splittie, all door hinges on the Bay were concealed internally, instead of standing proud in the airstream. This not only tidied up the vehicle's appearance, but went some way towards reducing drag. The Bay might have more closely resembled a house brick than the Splittie, but it was more aerodynamically efficient.

The differences between American- and European-spec Buses at this stage were minimal, the most visible from the outside being the circular amber reflectors below the cab doors, and the red ones behind the rear wheel arches. As the vehicle was developed, the differences would become more pronounced.

Single- and double-cab Pick-Ups differed from the mainstream models in the same manner as before. The air-intake engine louvres were necessarily placed horizontally in three banks of three, above the rear wheel arches. With its lockable flap, the Pick-Up's fuel filler was positioned on the right-hand side in front of the louvres, whereas the fuel filler on the other models

Making the most of so much extra interior space, Camper versions became more ingenious and diverse.

was much further back, behind the sliding door. The double-cab's rear side door, giving access to the rear passenger compartment, was hinged and opened in the conventional manner rather than sliding on runners.

A locker bed continued as a strong selling feature on the single-cab Pick-Ups, the top-hinged door having two horizontal louvres for ventilation. Both versions of the Pick-Up had conventional fold-down side flaps on the bed and a folding tailgate. The latter had a small aperture on each side, through which the tail-lamps and brake lights could be seen when the tailgate was in the down position. As with the Splittie, the bed had strips of hardwood attached to prevent the load from slipping.

Roof Panels

The high-roof Panelvan broke with tradition, in that the whole of the enlarged roof panel was made of fibreglass, and bonded to the standard Panelvan's metal body panels. The use of fibreglass was a surprising move from a manufacturer who had perfected the art of mass production.

A relatively new material, fibreglass still had something of a 'kit car' image in the minds of many, although Lotus boss Colin Chapman had been doing his best to dispel this for many years. Daimler-Benz had produced a GRP-bodied 300SL 'Gullwing' in the mid-1950s, but dismissed its use for the production car and reverted to steel and aluminium-alloy instead.

The great advantage for Volkswagen in producing the large Panelvan with a plastic roof was the huge reduction in weight provided by this non-rusting material. More than thirty years have passed since the feature was introduced, and time has shown that the designers made the right decision. A great many vehicles have plastic roofs today, and nowhere is this more in evidence

than in the world of Camper conversions. In using fibreglass, Volkswagen had achieved another first.

All other models in the range stuck to steel roof panels, and, in the case of the luxury Microbus, a sliding sunroof was provided as a standard fitment. On Panelvans, Kombis and the standard Microbus, this item was an extra-cost option; it is quite difficult to appreciate why the owner of a Panelvan would want one.

Wheels and Tyres

Initially, one of the few components – possibly the only one – to be carried over from the Splittie to the Bay was the domed hubcap, or more accurately, four of them. These were painted in white on all variants, except on the de luxe Microbus, which had chromed items. This was odd, as Volkswagen's other models – the Beetle, Type 3 saloon and Type 1 and Type 34 Karmann Ghias – all had flat chromed hubcaps by this stage.

Crossply tyres continued as standard, despite the ready availability of radials; whereas the rubber on the people-carrying Bus had a 6-ply rating, that on the Pick-Ups had the stronger 8-ply rating. From a driver's point of view, the ply rating difference made no difference; crossply tyres were crossply tyres, and they were still awful.

The Bay was an instant success in all markets. The larger body inevitably gave much more interior space, and camping converters were quick to capitalize on this. Commercial operators were delighted to be able to carry more cargo, while taxi and minicab businesses could take more luggage for passengers. Larger body panels gave signwriters and artists the possibility of exploiting more fully advertising opportunities on behalf of commercial operators. Hippies could also adorn their Bays with more flowers and peace slogans!

With its concealed door hinges and large one-piece panoramic windscreen, the Bay was altogether sleeker and able to penetrate the air more efficiently.

SAFETY AND COMFORT IN THE NEW WORLD

Safety Measures

When the first of the Split-Screens appeared in dealers' showrooms during the early 1950s, they were all basic utility vehicles, even the more luxuriously appointed Samba Microbus. By the mid-1960s, crash testing had become part of the development of prototypes, with data about the different effects of road-traffic accidents on drivers and passengers being collated by manufacturers. To a certain extent, this was dictated by legislation, but it did lead to vehicles that were better packaged. As more was discovered about safety, vehicles began to change in character very rapidly, and few manufacturers ever lost an opportunity to bring new safety-inspired componentry to the attention of the car-buying public.

Flatter door handles with trigger releases on the inside, rather than push-buttons on the outside, minimized the risk of injury to pedestrians, and the cab's rear-view mirror (encased in plastic rather than metal, as on the previous model) was designed to snap off in the event of a collision. These were small concessions, but important none the less.

Interior Improvements

The improvements to the interior were something of a revelation. As one commentator observed,

> The inside of the vehicle now has what can be called décor. While the law specified a certain amount of padding for each passenger, it wasn't just pasted on. Thorough planning went into the integration of the new vinyl upholstery and the padding to produce a beautiful modern interior.

About as far removed from the chrome and painted metal that characterized the interior of the Splittie, the inside of the Bay was softer and more welcoming. The seat squabs and backrests were larger, more comfortably shaped and covered in a hounddog tooth-pattern vinyl, which breathed more easily in warm weather. A plastic headlining was fitted in the cab across the range, and to the roof of the rear compartment of people-carrying vehicles.

Nine-seater versions had a separate driver's seat, which was adjustable through eight different positions front to rear. A

The front bumper on the Bay was flattened on both ends to form a cab step, the new fresh-air grille improved interior ventilation and the revised headlamps were from the Beetle parts bin. At first, the indicators were positioned below the headlamps.

double bench seat next to it had been similarly enlarged and re-shaped. It could also be adjusted, to two positions, by sliding the squab and backrest simultaneously. Some models had just two separate seats – one for the driver and one for the passenger – in the cab. A safety hook was provided on the rear wall of the cab for locking these seats into position, to prevent the backrest slamming forward in an accident.

The rear passenger seats were of the bench type, in two rows of three, the one nearest the sliding door having a folding backrest to allow for easier access to the rear bench. Seven-seater versions had a convenient walkway between the two single cab seats. In the rear there was a three-seater bench, and a two-seater in the centre, with grab handles provided on the wall behind the driver's seat. While the seats in the rear compartment of the de luxe Microbus were fixed, those in the Kombi and standard Microbus could be removed quickly by unscrewing the retaining butterfly nuts, instantly giving 177cu ft of cargo space.

Luxury Microbuses were beautifully trimmed, with the upholstery generally finished in two-tone colours and piped with a contrasting colour. All the interior panels were in a better-quality vinyl, and had alloy moulding strips mounted horizontally to divide the two-tone colours. Seat belts were provided for all passengers, and those travelling in the luxury Microbus enjoyed the additional advantage of armrests on the outside of the seats.

Ventilation and Heating

The armrests on the cab doors were particularly well designed and innovative; they included a channel below them, which could be used for ducting fresh air collected from a distribution box below the dashboard to

A motorized hold-all that served as a fishing lodge, boardroom, hotel, taxi and family hack, the Bay was an ideal means of escape. The sliding side door was also a huge bonus.

outlets in the rear passenger compartment. A real bonus for passengers was the greatly improved system for distributing cold and warm air throughout the whole of the interior.

The system still relied on heat exchangers built around the exhaust pipes, but the two defroster outlets on top of the dashboard performed an admirable job of clearing the large windscreen. Two heater vents were provided under the dashboard, one between the cab seats, and two further ones below the rear seat in the passenger compartment. The latter were controlled by handles on the vents, whereas all the others were operated by sliding levers on the dashboard. Swivel vents for cool air were also positioned on each side of the dashboard.

For those who remained less than impressed by the standard heating system, an auxiliary Eberspächer petrol heater was available as an extra-cost option. This worked well when it worked at all, but was an amazingly expensive piece of equipment of which relatively few owners availed themselves.

The Dashboard

Until the advent of the 1303 Beetle in 1973, the saloon's painted metal dashboard and minimal instrumentation had become a hallmark of the austerity for which these cars had become famous. The Split-Screen Bus had been equally 'minimalist'; it was a feature that Bus and Beetle owners had come to expect, and that many had grown to love.

All this changed with the Bay-Window, which had a totally new dashboard, padded and covered in a non-reflective vinyl. All switchgear was in flat, soft plastic and clearly labelled. This was in stark contrast to the Splittie's hard plastic switchgear, which, elegant as it looked, had been deemed to be potentially lethal by American legislation. The Bay's instrument binnacle was also shrouded to prevent reflections in the windscreen.

All the gauges were made and supplied by VDO, as before, and comprised a dial on the left for fuel in the top segment and warning lights for the dynamo, headlamp high beam, oil pressure, side lights and indicators in the lower sector. A speedometer sat in the centre and there was a circular blanking plate to the right for fitting a clock. This was an extra-cost option, except on the de luxe Microbus, on which it was standard.

As the new 1600cc engine was without the throttle governor that had seen service on the last of the Splitties, a tachometer might have been more useful. However, Volkswagen viewed such devices with great scepticism – tachometers were associated with a sporting image, and this was something from which the company had always distanced itself – and did not include one.

As a radio was always an extra-cost option, the centre of the dashboard had a small removable plate. Below this was a sliding ashtray with a padded face. In place of a conventional floor-mounted handbrake lever, the

Shining Panelvans and Pick-Ups at the London Motor Show, before the usual years of use and abuse, which so often led them to end their days ...

Bay had an 'umbrella'-type below the ash-tray; this always took a little getting used to.

A glovebox of a good size (still known by this name so many years after motorists stopped wearing gloves) was provided, along with a padded grab handle on the passenger's side. Buses in some markets were not provided with glovebox lids – one of Volkswagen's little 'penny-pinching' exercises that continues to be criticized in some quarters.

The large plastic steering wheel was to a new two-spoke design and deeply dished. Although it was comfortable to use and indestructible, the steering wheel was certainly not good-looking. The Bay's fusebox was located under the dashboard, and fitted with a clear plastic cover which, like the switchgear, was clearly labelled with identification symbols. This was the kind of attention to detail that had been lacking in the

Splittie range, and was particularly appreciated by owners when a fuse needed changing on a cold, dark night.

Another new innovation was the mounting of the brake fluid reservoir under the left-hand side of the dashboard, where its fluid level could be checked more easily. Dual-circuit braking was also new, and a failure in the system would immediately illuminate a red warning light on the dashboard. Pressing this light inwards also lit it up for the purpose of testing both the bulb and the electric circuit; it was operated by a small piston inside the housing of the master cylinder.

PRESS REACTION

All in all, Volkswagen had done a really good job of creating a new Bus. It retained

... like this. Scrapheaps can provide rich hunting grounds for restorers.

some of the character of the Splittie but at the same time catered for the requirements of customers, and of the legislation that demanded so much more from motor manufacturers. As usual, the proof of the pudding was in the eating; journalists openly raved about the Bay.

From the driving seat, it felt light years ahead of its rivals and, of course, of the model that it had just replaced. The *American World Car Guide* remarked on it as follows:

The VW Bus stands in a class of its own. It's such a practical shape for carrying people and their recreational accoutrement that, unfortunately, the tendency is to cram more into it than its engine will handle. In the two weeks we lived with it, the Bus did its job which was to take us wherever we wanted to go. The fact that it required twenty more minutes to make the run from Los Angeles to San Diego seemed quite unimportant when, the next day, we

purchased the family Christmas tree and carried all seven feet of it, branches unbroken with the top protruding through the sunroof. You can't do that in a Cadillac, despite its 375 horsepower.

Like its predecessor, the Bay was a classless means of transport that appealed to a greater cross-section of society than any other vehicle, with the possible exception of the Beetle. Volkswagen really had pulled it off again.

HANDLING THE PACE

Transverse torsion bar springing and parallel trailing arms were retained front and rear, with the torsion bar tubes attached as an integral part of the chassis. Pioneered by Porsche on the 356 sports car, non-detachable tubes made for a much stronger, stiffer chassis. Like so many manufacturers at this time, Volkswagen could easily have opted for coil springs and MacPherson struts. These were much lighter, easier and cheaper to make, took up less space and gave a potentially improved turning circle, but old habits die hard. Coil springs would have to wait until the third-generation Buses.

At the front, king and link pins were replaced by maintenance-free ball joints, and reduction gearboxes were no longer a feature of the rear hubs. This latter change had the effect of increasing the sprung/unsprung weight ratio, which not only improved ride quality, but 'stuck' the wheels to the road more securely.

The two-spoke steering wheel was deeply dished and typically on the large side, and fresh air was ducted to the rear passenger area through channels below the door armrests. Wooden gear knobs were fitted to Microbuses in some markets.

Cab comfort was much improved with bigger, better-shaped seats, easy-to-clean vinyl upholstery, vinyl headlining, and a padded dashboard for enhanced safety.

Because of criticism of Volkswagen's long-held belief in the virtue of swing axles, as a means of independent wheel suspension at the rear, the Bay's system was substantially revised.

During the 1950s and 60s, there were many people who disliked Volkswagens intensely. They saw the Bus and the Beetle as products of the old Nazi regime – some even dubbing them 'Hitler's revenge' – and they rarely missed an opportunity to come down on 'problems' with the rear suspension. They argued time and again that it was potentially dangerous. Under extremely hard cornering, a sudden change in the camber of a rear wheel could cause the swing axle to travel through the maximum length of its arc, causing the wheel in turn to adopt an acute angle under the axle. With the rear weight bias of the engine and transmission, the theoretical result was sudden tail-end breakaway and instant inversion on to the vehicle's roof. In practice, this was extremely rare, if it ever occurred at all; the road speed likely to lead to such a situation would only have been achieved by a driver close to insanity.

However, in the face of continued pressure from the anti-Volkswagen brigade, Volkswagen relented and made changes. Seeking counsel from Porsche, whose 911 model was already a couple of years into production, they continued the Bus with what were, in effect, swing axles. However, the slimmer driveshafts – no longer contained within axle tubes – incorporated a constant velocity universal joint on their ends. These joints were each able to absorb a maximum of 1in (2.5cm) in axial play. As well as the parallel trailing arms on each side, which coped with acceleration and deceleration forces, diagonal links in front of the gearbox were welded on to the torsion bar tubes, and swivelled on lateral rubber-bushed axes. Sturdy pieces of metal, these links were attached to the rear axle at the wheel hubs.

This new arrangement ensured that the rear wheel remained upright, irrespective of cornering loads, and regardless of the weight carried on board. In conjunction with the front anti-roll bar, and increased track of 2½in (6.25cm), the effect of these changes on roadholding and handling was dramatic. The Bus had been transformed from a fun and inherent over-steerer into a clinical under-steerer.

The purists, who took great pride in their ability to conduct a Splittie quickly and safely without worrying about arriving too soon in the next world, and who enjoyed the delights of 'opposite lock', were not impressed. Some saw the new arrangement as the ultimate heresy, representing the beginnings of a 'nanny' motoring society. Others, however, appreciated its safety aspects.

The double-cab Pick-Up had a conventional hinged door, for access to the rear passenger area.

Plain hardboard provided interior panelling in the double-cab, and there were painted metal pillars; it lacked the locker bed of its single-cab sister, but ample storage space was provided below the seat.

With fewer corners in their huge road system, customers in North America – Volkswagen's biggest export market – were not particularly bothered one way or the other, but they liked the Bay's improved ride quality and sharper handling and steering characteristics. Strong sidewinds continued to deflect the Bus from the straight and narrow, but not to the same extent that it had with the Splittie. This lent weight to the notion that all modifications were in the nature of real improvements.

Not everyone enjoyed handling the Bus in strong winds, though. Writing in *Road & Track*, Dick O'Kane commented,

> For all this common sense, economy and space, one pays one's dues. For instance,

consider the size and shape of the thing. It has all the aerodynamic purity of a sheet-iron cowshed, and if you like the sedan in a crosswind, you'll just love the truck! It doesn't just meander around the road in wind, either. It blows helplessly around like a big empty box, it can meander clean off the road in a trice, and sudden bullish changes into the other lane are commonplace – but, here, at last, after all these years, you get a chance to frighten all the oncoming traffic.

Firstly, it speaks volumes for the Bus that *Road & Track* magazine, which more usually associated itself with 'upmarket' sports cars, was once again testing a Volkswagen. Secondly, although the article was written tongue firmly in cheek, it did capture that part of the Transporter's endearing character that had not been completely eliminated by Volkswagen's engineering department. O'Kane used his test vehicle for a long trip through North Africa, as did so many Bus people during the 1960s and 70s, and soon discovered the value of torsion bar suspension. As he remarked,

> Just drive until you find a place with a free view. And if the roadside doesn't suit you, leave it – the People's Truck stands tall and proud on skinny tyres, most of its vitals are tucked up out of reach of those big, pointy rocks, and it can take you pretty far afield without damage or embarrassment to itself or its load.

The suspension system gave the Bay its ability to withstand abuse in harsh places like North Africa – possibly its greatest strength. It would keep going long after conventional rivals had given up, and this is just one reason why so many Bay-Windows are still in daily use now.

Roger Pascoe, a leading light in the British Volkswagen scene, has a familiar story. In the early 1970s, he was a mechanic for a motor-cycle racing team and travelled throughout Continental Europe from race to race. On one occasion, it fell to him to drive the team's Bedford truck, with all the spanners and motor-cycle spare parts on board, to a race meeting in Sweden. The truck suffered a mechanical breakdown, requiring new engine parts. These were not available in any Scandinavian country, and Pascoe had to fly home to Britain, buy the necessary bits and pieces, and fly back to Sweden. After this harrowing and expensive experience, he sold the Bedford and bought a Bay-Window double-cab Pick-Up truck. He never looked back, never experienced mechanical problems again, and has owned air-cooled Volkswagens ever since.

POWER INCREASE

The engine remained in its normal place slung out in the tail, mated to the four-speed all-synchromesh gearbox, which sat directly in front of it. There was, however, a little more power available. By this time, the Type 3 saloon's power unit had grown from 1500cc to 1600cc, so it was a natural decision to slot this unit into the Transporter. Once again, it had to be modified to fit, and this was achieved by removing the Type 3's crankshaft-mounted cooling fan and alloy shroud, replacing it with the more traditional vertical fan and fan housing mounted on top of the crankcase.

Capacity

With a bore and stroke of 85.5 × 69mm, the overall capacity worked out at 1,584cc, producing 47bhp at 4,000rpm. For the majority of markets, the new engine had an increased compression ratio of 7.7:1 but, for countries where poor-quality fuels predominated, 6.6:1 low-compression engines with concave piston tops were available.

American-spec Transporters had safety-inspired side reflectors front and rear.

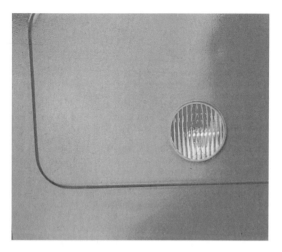

Apertures in the tailgate on Pick-Ups allowed the tail-lamps to be seen when the tailgate was down.

Maximum speed was officially quoted at 65mph (104km/h), despite the lack of the throttle governor fitted to the old 1500 version. There was no improvement in acceleration, because of the vehicle's increased weight, but fuel consumption worked out at a reasonable 23–25mpg (11.3–12.3l/100km), depending upon driving style, load and conditions.

Built to the same flat-four air-cooled design as all previous engines, the 1600 was a bored-out version of the 1500. It was frustrating for owners that fuel was still dispensed to the combustion chambers through a small-bore inlet manifold, and a single inlet port in each of the cylinder heads. Twin ports would have done nicely as a way of increasing power but, for the time being, Volkswagen slogged on in the same old way.

Carburettor

A single Solex carburettor continued to be fitted, although the Type 3 saloon's twin carburettor set-up would have been preferable, in view of the increased payload. Small

differences began to appear, however, between carburettor types at this stage to cater for the demands of different markets. Because of increasingly stringent exhaust emissions regulations, American-spec models got the most complex of the new carburettors – the Solex 30 PICT 2. Designed to measure the flow of fuel more precisely, there was a vacuum-controlled dashpot that left the throttle slightly open on deceleration. This made for cleaner and fuller combustion of the fuel/air mixture.

The Solex PICT 1, PICT 3 and 34 PICT 3 Solexes saw service in other markets, except North America, and differed in the smallest details. Also, to reduce the time it took for the fuel/air mixture to warm up, the weight loaded valve in the oil bath air cleaner was replaced by a valve controlled by a cable connected to the thermostat located at the bottom of the engine.

Set-Up

Because of the additional weight of the new power unit, it was supported by a crossmember under the engine. This was attached to the chassis on both sides, and was similar in arrangement to the one employed on the Type 3 saloons. In conjunction with a stronger mounting at the front of the gearbox, this set-up very much improved the engine's resistance to the forces of torque and vibration.

Success and Sales

The Bay weighed 1,000lb (455kg) more than the Beetle, and was powered by a similarly modest number of horses, so that driving it at a reasonable pace was something of an art, requiring the utmost skill and patience. Reaching the benchmark speed of 60mph (96km/h) took a minimum of 37 seconds, a figure in the car world matched only by the

Dutch-built, belt-driven Daf; overtaking demanded anticipatory powers of the most concentrated kind.

This was hardly the point of the Bus, however, and journalists acknowledged the vehicle – new engine or not – for what it was. There was no shortage of rival machines by this stage, but the Volkswagen, despite its diminutive engine, reigned supreme.

Don McDonald, writing in the 1970 *World Car Guide*, commented as follows:

If the Greenbrier, a slab-nosed, rear engine equippage produced by Chevrolet in the

Versatile workhorse or not, the Bus was most appreciated by owners and journalists alike from behind the wheel. Few failed to be impressed by the Bus's car-like road manners.

early 1960s were still around in modernized form, a tester would have at least some basis from which to take the measure of a Volkswagen Station Wagon. The Greenbrier was an imitator and follower but like VW, design emphasis favoured passenger rather than commercial versions. The current crop of domestic front-engined boxcars are overly expensive, gussied-up trucks.

Until 1974–75, when sales began to tail off, Volkswagen made around a quarter of a million Buses annually. In the first few years of its life, the 1600 engine proved itself to be as trusty and dependable as its predecessors but, by the early 1970s, 47bhp was just not sufficient. Criticism from journalists and owners became vociferous. Things would have to change, and rapidly, if the Bus was going to keep pace with its competitors.

GEARING UP

Although the Bay's gearbox was similar in design to the previous one-piece tunnel-type transmission introduced in May 1959, it had

Staff at Wolfsburg and Hanover continued working around the clock to keep up with demand, despite powerful competition from rival manufacturers.

Although the Splittie's 1500 engine was good, it was under-powered, and many hoped that Volkswagen would take the opportunity to consign it to the scrapheap in favour of real power.

a separate alloy bellhousing containing the single 200mm dry-plate clutch. A strong and exceptionally complex piece of equipment, the synchromesh was as faultless as ever, and the revised ratios allowed for more relaxed cruising. The ratios were: first 3.80:1, second 2.06:1, third 1.26:1, top 0.89:1, reverse 3.61:1, and 4.125:1 for the final-drive ratio.

The hypoid ring and pinion gearing had a 10mm offset, and the differential housing was carried in tapered roller bearings, which gave slightly quieter running. Changing up and down through the gearbox was not, however, the usual pleasurable Volkswagen experience. The gear lever had been increased in length by 1¾in (about 4.5cm) and felt vague as a result. With wear, the stick would flop around, and make a noise rather like a fax machine.

On the other hand, the clutch was commendably light, and even improved in feel after the change from a coil spring plate to the diaphragm type, in August 1970. In view of the fact that so many Transporters found customers living in remote areas, where roads were either rudimentary or non-existent, it was a great pity that Volkswagen never made a production version of the five four-wheel drive prototypes that the company built in 1978.

For the majority of customers, however, the excellent traction afforded by the weight of the engine and transmission was sufficient on most types of terrain. For those who ventured far off the beaten track, a limited-slip differential was available, at extra cost, right from the beginning of Bay-Window production.

STEERING AND STOPPING

Many of those who took to the Bay so eagerly did so because driving one was like driving a car. It was much easier than so many light commercials at that time, which had heavy controls, back-breakingly uncomfortable seats, and excessive road and mechanical noise in the cabin. The Transporter was different from these kinds of vehicle in all respects, but particularly in its steering. Light and reasonably precise, the Transporter's steering allowed a confident driver

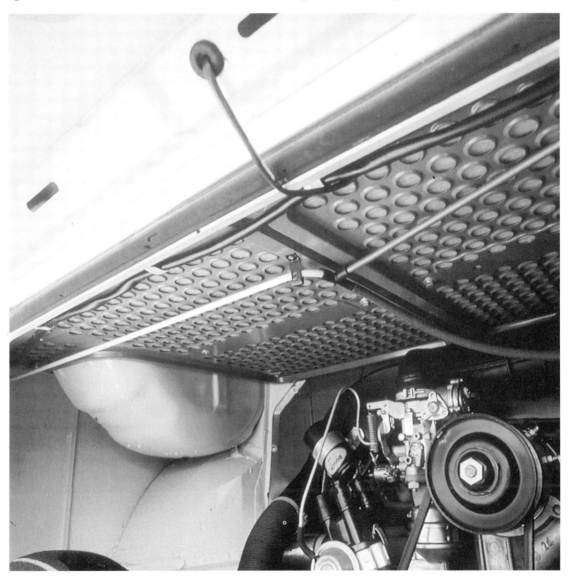

The new 1600 engine was to the same design as the 1500, and felt lively by comparison, but had no more to offer than a paltry 47bhp.

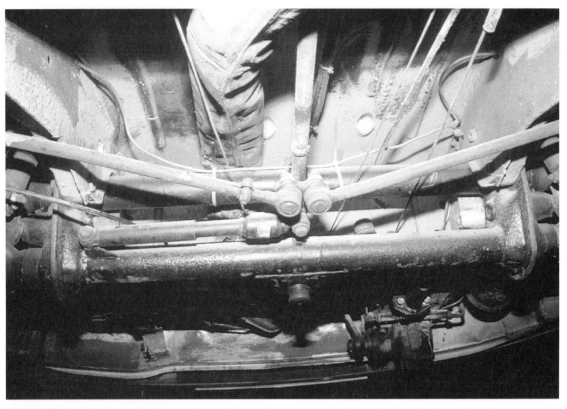

Porsche's torsion-bar springing with parallel trailing arms was used front and rear – there was no good reason to change it at this stage.

to place the vehicle exceptionally well in the blindest of corners. With 2.8 turns from lock to lock, it was relatively low-geared, even if the 39ft (12m) turning circle was a trifle on the broad side.

The small amount of play in the steering, present in all Bays, was largely down to the complexities of the indirect steering system. As the *American World Car Guide* commented,

> You've got to remember that the front wheels are behind you and not start a sharp turn until you protrude about half the vehicle's length into the intersection. If the corner happens to be adorned with an obstacle, such as the gatepost of a drive-

way, rather expensive alterations are made in the big sliding door on the right side.

The front axle sat behind the steering column, which necessitated a series of link arms situated between the steering box and tie-rods of unequal length. To the same worm-and-peg design as previously, the steering gearbox had been tried and tested over many years, and was known to suffer from serious wear at around 130,000 miles (208,000km). A new worm-and-roller box replaced it from August 1972, in the interests of greater longevity.

When Volkswagen launched the much-lamented 1500 Beetle in August 1966, one of its strongest features was the ATE front disc brakes. Smooth, powerful and effective, they transformed the car's stopping power. However, curiously, the Bay continued with drums at all four corners. Front and rear drums were 250mm in diameter with 55mm wide front linings, and 45mm wide linings at the rear. These worked reasonably well, but were far from perfect. With a heavy load on board, long braking distances were required, especially in the wet, because of the inherent tendency of a rear-engined vehicle to lock its front wheels. Porsche had discovered this with their works rally 911s during the late 1960s, and so had Alpine, with their pretty fibreglass-bodied A110 rally cars a little later but, until the advent of ABS, little could be done about it.

Journalists and owners accepted this facet of the Bay's character as part of every-day Volkswagen motoring. They became less impressed, however, with the vagaries of drums when the Bus was also treated to a pair of power-assisted front discs, from August 1970. The ability of the Transporter to 'sprint' to 60mph (96km/h) from a standing start may not have been impressive but, with the discs, the vehicle's talent for decelerating from this speed was amazing.

Even under fierce pedal application, there was instant 'bite', no directional instability, and a minimal tendency for the front wheels to lock. With a 20 per cent increase in the width of the rear linings at the same time – up to 55mm – and a brake force regulator in the rear of the two independent braking circuits, which acted as an anti-skid device, the days of rear-wheel locking were just about over.

American Road Test magazine commented as follows:

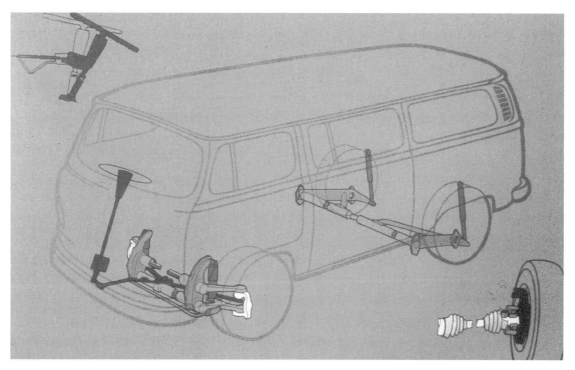

Maintenance-free ball joints were fitted at the front for the first time, and the driveshafts were 'double-jointed' to improve roadholding, but reduction hubs were not featured.

The designers had taken a calculated risk in getting away from the strong image associated with the classic Splittie, and it worked.

It's almost as though the proverbial great hand is reaching out to take hold of the car. The numbers bear out the feeling, with the stopping distance of 167ft [50m] from 60mph [96km/h] being equivalent to a deceleration rate of about 23ft/sec or .72g.

The testers discovered from their recorded data that the average deceleration rate from 60mph (96km/h) to rest was twice the rate of acceleration from standstill to 60mph.

This phenomenal braking ability was undoubtedly aided by the road wheels, which were increased in width from 4.5J to 5.5J, and also perforated with a series of circular vents to help cooling.

WINGS CLIPPED

During 1967, Volkswagen ran into a spot of bother. The company had bestowed a name – the Clipper – for the first time on the range-topping Microbus. This was unusual because all models had been known at the factory by a Type number. The Beetle (never an official Volkswagen name) was the Type 1, and the Bus the Type 2.

British aircraft company BOAC (now defunct) had been running a Clipper Class service to North America for some time, and objected to Volkswagen's use of the Clipper name for the Microbus. After a short dispute between the two companies, Volkswagen conceded defeat, and the vehicle was renamed Microbus L. Officially, the Clipper

As interest in the Bay-Window grew towards the end of the 1960s, the Split-Screens faded gracefully into history.

name had lasted for around twelve months but, interestingly, it stuck, and Bay-Window enthusiasts on both sides of the Atlantic continue to refer to the luxury Microbus by this name.

A VEHICLE FOR THE ANTI-ESTABLISHMENT

Beginning with a completely clean sheet of paper for the design of the Bay-Window, Volkswagen's designers were aware of the risk they were taking in getting so far away

from the classic image of the Split-Screen range. Volkswagen admitted openly that the Bay's overall styling package made it look rather like a 'loaf of bread on wheels', but it was at least fresh and functional. By a quirk of fate, the Bay, too, would come to be regarded as a timeless classic.

Clearly, it would never appeal to 'speed merchants', and its upright driving position, with pedals rising from the floor and an almost horizontal steering wheel, made those for whom comfort was a high priority think twice. (Incidentally, modern designers

Between 1970 and 1973, when this pristine Microbus was built, sales figures constantly peaked above 250,000 units per year, another triumph for the 'box on wheels' philosophy.

have improved multi-purpose vehicles immeasurably by putting the steering wheel in a more car-like position, putting an end to the backache brought on by the horizontal ones of yesteryear.)

Despite a few niggling drawbacks, the Bay served as an outstanding commuting, camping or delivery vehicle that boasted reasonable running costs, low depreciation, dependable mechanicals, and reasonable levels of comfort. It was also considerably safer than the model it replaced. People from all walks of life – from hippies to High Court judges, old and young alike – all around the globe embraced it, making it a huge success.

In parts of North America and Europe (although to a lesser extent in Britain), the Bay developed something of a controversial image. It came to be seen by some as a vehicle for the anti-establishment rebel. As Dick O'Kane wrote in his humorous road test in *Road & Track*,

> Yet another hassle you learn to live with is cops. You'd think that a vehicle capable of nothing more dangerous than a brisk trundle would be left alone by the fuzz, but it is not so. Because of its nature – cheap practicality with a highly mobile view – the Volksie van is rapidly becoming the Official Vehicle of the International Counter-Culture, which means that young people with hair, bright clothing, rather loose schedules and other such threats to God and Country have taken to it. To the average cop, then, that big tin box full of hair gasping up the hill is nothing less than the Main Stash – a thousand-kilo brick of Panama Red disguised as a Volksie van, with windows and doors and freaks painted on it and 'wow', we're all gonna make sergeant.

Those who served on the Volkswagen board were not especially bothered that some of their clients imbibed excessively, and smoked illegal substances. They simply continued happily totting up the year-on-year profits from increasing sales. Profits were ploughed directly back into the company for future prosperity (unlike one or two of their British rivals, who squandered taxpayers' money on one disastrous project after another).

4 Ebb and Flow in the Bay

INTO THE 1970s

Volkswagen's Cars

After the death of Heinz Nordhoff in 1968, development of Volkswagen's products began to speed up. The Bus had been, and would continue to be, a clear market leader, but Volkswagen could not afford to be complacent. By the end of the 1960s, rival manufacturers had caught up, and some were threatening to overtake them. Cheaper products from Japan were gaining an increasing share of the market. The Beetle continued to sell well, peaking at 1.2 million units in 1971, but nobody was more surprised than Volkswagen's sales and marketing departments. By the mid-1960s, the company had consumed NSU, but its revolutionary and futuristic rotary-engined RO80, intended as a new 'flagship', proved to be unreliable, and sales quickly died away.

The K70 saloon – another intended replacement for the Beetle – was launched in 1970. This, the company's first production front-wheel drive, water-cooled saloon was one of the world's most notorious sales disasters. A powerful, spacious, comfortable and, by the standards of the day, entirely conventional saloon, it should have been a success. However, in trying to get away from the Beetle, and launch the company into a modern world, Volkswagen had made a mistake. Much of their success had been based on their products being very different from those of other companies. To the car-buying public, a conventional saloon with a Volkswagen badge was a contradiction in terms. Incidentally, Porsche would suffer from the same problem, when it ventured into the world of 'conventional' front-engined sports cars, with the launch of the 928 model in the mid-1970s.

Volkswagen's Commercials

Those responsible for Volkswagen's car department were in a state of panic, but the commercial division remained quietly confident that the proven soundness of the Transporter's design would stand them in good stead. Development of the Bus continued in the same vein as always. The designers looked carefully at each component, searching for ways in which the smallest improvements could be made, and these were incorporated year on year. As usual, major changes were announced in August, at the start of each new model year, while minor modifications were made throughout the year.

The majority of changes were subtle; Volkswagen refused to join in the industry trend for producing a 'facelifted' model each year, just to appease every whim of the dealers. Customers appreciated this approach, and production increased from 810 units per day throughout 1967, to 1,092 by 1970. Westfalia continued as Volkswagen's officially appointed Camper converter, and,

Although German tuning company Okrasa had been making twin-port cylinder heads since the 1950s, it took Volkswagen until 1970 to do the same. These engines were outwardly distinguishable by the 'Siamesed' cast-alloy inlet manifolds. Power output increased to 50bhp.

although it was relatively expensive, this model sold exceptionally well in North America. Elsewhere, independent converters took advantage of, and capitalized on, the new model's additional space. Their efforts contributed hugely to the general popularity of the Transporter. In Britain, convertor's names, including Dormobile and Devon, became synonymous with the Bus, almost in the same way as Hoover had become the accepted name for the vacuum cleaner.

Between its debut in August 1967, and 1970, when the three-millionth Transporter was produced, the vehicle remained virtually unchanged. The company's publicity literature announced that it offered 'More safety, more comfort', but the changes for

the 1970 model year went largely unnoticed. In fact, the body had been made more rigid, the inner door frames had been strengthened, to improve passenger and driver protection against side impacts, and a collapsible steering column had been fitted. The circular side reflectors on US-spec vehicles were changed for larger, rectangular items, supposedly to make them more visible – and therefore adding another safety feature – but doing little for the vehicle's aesthetics. (Incidentally, at this time, the Americans, who had become obsessive about road safety, continued to accept the terrible loss of life in their senseless war in Vietnam. This irony was not missed by antiwar protesters, and the image of the Bus as a symbol of peace was further enhanced.)

At the base of the engine, the central nut, which had previously sat in the centre of the oil strainer plate, was dropped. This was very annoying, especially for mechanics; without the nut, oil changes could only be carried out by removing the entire strainer plate, and this necessitated the removal of the six retaining nuts around the outside of the component.

Another Hole in the Head

As well as the fitting of disc brakes at the front and wider wheels, August 1970 saw something of a 'U-turn' in the engineering department. It was believed for many years that there were well-defined limits to the tuning possibilities of an air-cooled engine. Respected engineers had argued that the maximum power to be extracted from the 1200 engine, for example, was around 75bhp. Above this figure, they claimed that the engine became unreliable and short-lived. And they were slow to change their ideas.

In 1969, Porsche astonished the motor-racing establishment with the launch of their hastily built 917 sports racing car. Originally fitted with a 4.5-litre, air-cooled, horizontally opposed 12-cylinder engine – there was also a stillborn 16-cylinder unit – producing around 500bhp, the 917 proved beyond all reasonable doubt that power output was limited only by the amount of money that could be thrown at development. Indeed, in twin-turbo Can-Am guise, the 917's engine developed no less than 1,100bhp!

Professor Porsche's grandson, Ferdinand Piech, once remarked that 'the target was to keep the Beetle competitive in the marketplace by showing the limit of air-cooled engines'. Volkswagen supported the ambitious 917 project, and Piech confessed that the Stuttgart concern could not have succeeded without this. The links between the two companies were as close as ever, and

While all other models in the Volkswagen line-up had flat hubcaps from the mid-1960s, the Bus continued to use drum brakes and domed hubcaps right up until 1970.

there was little excuse for doing nothing about the under-powered 1600cc Volkswagen unit. The future of both the Beetle and the Bus depended on it.

The German tuning company Okrasa had been producing additional power for Volkswagens since the 1950s – twin-port cylinder heads had played a major role in this – and Volkswagen agreed at last that a revised

When front disc brakes were introduced in 1970, the 14in wheels had circular perforations to aid cooling and dissipate heat, and the more modern flat hubcaps were fitted. The wheels were painted silver across the range.

cylinder head would provide a practical solution to the perceived problem of finding additional power. By and large, the revised heads were to much the same design as before, except that, in place of a single inlet port, there were two, positioned side by side. This not only made the engine run more smoothly, and 'breathe' more efficiently, it also increased power output to 50bhp (DIN) at a maximum 4,000rpm. Unfortunately, the 1,584cc barrels and pistons and single Solex carburettor were retained, but it was at least a step in the right direction.

With the slight increase in power came a slight increase in cylinder head temperature, and efficient cooling became even more critical than before. To help dissipate heat more quickly and efficiently, the oil cooler was made of aluminium-alloy instead of steel, and the fan housing was modified in shape at the front, to allow for better collection and distribution of cool air over the engine. The exhaust tailbox was also modified to allow spent gases to escape more quickly. Because of the additional port in each cylinder head, the inlet manifold was modified, with a single pipe dividing into two cast-alloy pipes at the heads.

For owners who were used to the Transporter's comparatively mediocre performance, the revised engine was a great improvement over the single-port 1600 unit. Certain members of the press, though, were still not convinced. In a back-to-back test between the VW Bus and three American transporters, published in the April 1971 issue of *Motor Trend* magazine, the writer commented as follows:

Despite the addition of disc brakes and a minuscule power increase in the '71 van, VW still persists with their 96cu in engine – less than one-third of the size of the engines available in any of the Detroit designed vans we drove. So while the '71 minibus radiates the glories-of-a-smaller-outside, nearly-as-big-inside accommodation, more manoeuvrability, better brakes, far superior control, no rattles, easier steering, greater gas mileage, lower upkeep, higher re-sale and rock-bottom investment – the thing still needs more performance.

During 1970, Volkswagen sold 65,000 Transporters in North America, which was well ahead of Dodge, but behind Chevrolet and Ford. The big front-engined, rear-wheel drive American V8s were all but useless on ice, snow and deep mud, but sales figures demonstrated that power was beginning to win the day.

The writer of the *Motor Trend* report had, however, concluded, 'now, if Detroit could only offer VW's quality at a competitive price...'. Transporters continued to sell well – the success of the Porsche 917 was clearly influential – and the message about more power from critical journalists was at last beginning to hit home.

TYPE 4 TRANSPLANT

For the 1972 model year, the entire range, with the exception of the Pick-Ups, came with the option of the 1.7-litre engine that had powered Volkswagen's Type 4 saloon since its launch in 1968. North America was unique in that Pick-Ups were also offered with this unit. A much more complex piece of engineering, closer to Porsche thinking than Volkswagen's, it produced a genuinely useful 66bhp at 4,800rpm.

Overall capacity worked out at 1,679cc with a bore and stroke of 90×60mm, and, although it was to the same flat-four design, it was so substantially different from the previous 1600 engine that few parts were interchangeable between the two units. The crankcase was considerably stronger, the oil galleries larger, for better lubrication, and

For the 1972 model year, the Type 4 saloon's twin-carburettor 1679cc engine, with the cooling fan mounted on the nose of the crankshaft, was available as an option.

the valve stems were filled with sodium to aid cooling.

In place of the asthmatic single Solex carburettor was a pair of Solex 34 PDSITs. These not only helped the vehicle to a 'sizzling' top speed of 76mph (122km/h), but also eliminated the age-old problem of the single carburettor and inlet manifold icing up in cold weather. Although not on a par with that of the American V8s, acceleration was much more acceptable, 60mph (96km/h) being achieved from rest in a minimum of around 22 seconds.

The appearance of the power unit was also changed dramatically. Following Type 3 and 4 saloon practice, the cooling fan was enlarged, and mounted on the end of the crankshaft at the rear of the engine. Made

of aluminium-alloy, the shroud, or fan housing, bolted over the fan and the top of the engine, and was made much flatter. (This gave rise to the unit's nickname of 'suitcase'.) As a result of these changes, the Bosch coil and dynamo, and the oil-filler neck sat much lower in the engine bay, and were more accessible for servicing.

Access to the carburettors, sparking plugs and distributor was not so good, which is why these models had a quickly removable hatch fitted in the luggage bay above the engine. In addition, in a really up-to-date touch, both the Bus and Beetle had an electronic diagnostic socket fitted in the engine bay. This improved the lot of the mechanic; when connected to a machine, it could reveal faults with the engine more easily than the traditional method of a test drive by a mechanic with sensitive ears.

Because of this engine's extra weight, it was secured to the gearbox with eight bolts, instead of the more traditional four. In addition, although the gear ratios were not changed, the transmission casing was beefed up and made stronger than the one it replaced.

In some respects, though by no means in all its features, the 1.7-litre engine was Volkswagen's best effort to date. However, the introduction of the electronic diagnostic equipment signalled the beginning of the end of a time when owners could endlessly 'tinker', and maintain their vehicles at home.

Many motoring writers gave the new engine the thumbs up. Some even reported that it was possible to get wheelspin moving away from rest – previously unheard of with a stock Bus – while others enthused about its improved ability to climb steep hills. With

a 23 per cent gain in performance, it felt lively through the gears, yet gave reasonable fuel mileage of 23mpg (12.3l/100km) at a constant 60mph (96km/h).

The engine had, however, one major disadvantage. It was fitted with a speed limiter, which restricted it to a maximum of 5,400rpm; although this could be inconvenient if it cut in during a rapid overtaking manoeuvre, it did prevent expensive high-speed detonation of the moving parts.

Naturally, the extra performance also led to a slight increase in mechanical noise. To counteract the effect on passengers, thicker sound-proofing materials were employed on the floor and on the interior body panels.

TREADING CAREFULLY

On all models, except the Pick-Up, radial-ply tyres replaced the traditional crossply

The simple and attractive tail-lamps fitted to the last of the Splitties and early Bays were no longer considered safe by the early 1970s.

These tall vertical stacks, fitted from August 1971, included built-in reversing lamps, but did little to improve the Bus's looks.

The traditional crescent-shaped air-intake louvres behind the rear side windows were adequate to serve the 1600 engine, but ...

... were enlarged considerably when the 1700 engine was introduced.

tyres – not before time, some argued. Radials had been fitted as standard on the luxury Microbus from the start of Bay-Window production. However, when the meaty Continental 185×14s saw service on the Panelvan, they increased noise levels in the cabin further and, incredibly, drew criticism from road testers. Crossply tyres had dogged cars and commercials for years.

The introduction of the much safer radial improved the Bus's handling immeasurably, and for journalists to gripe about the 'whooshing' noise at high speed was really to miss the point. Owners, on the other hand, were grateful to have a vehicle that

would travel in a straight line, without the need to correct the steering at every irregularity in the road surface. Cornering speeds also increased greatly and, with the front disc brakes, stopping quickly was made a much safer affair.

Bodywork changes were related to the increase in engine power and tyre width. The front wheel arches were flared and matched those at the rear, and the air-intake louvres behind the rear side windows were enlarged, for the purpose of feeding larger quantities of cold air through to the cooling fan.

The South African publication *Car*, in its June 1972 road test of the Kombi version, reckoned it to be the best Volkswagen

Transporter to date. It concluded as follows:

> It sets new standards in performance and safety, and is a most endearing family vehicle. A family of six can get lost inside its big interior, yet its overall dimensions are those of a medium VW car. Every inch of overall length and width is used to provide travelling and living space – which makes good sense for families who like to get around in comfort.

THE 1973 MODEL YEAR

All Quiet in Hanover

Although Volkswagen launched a revised model in August 1972 for the 1973 model year, the changes – apart from the 'crumple zone' in the cab floor, designed to collapse in a pre-determined manner in the event of a frontal impact – were of relatively little consequence.

Heavier and stronger, energy-absorbing bumpers were fitted front and rear, and the front ones no longer had their outer ends flattened to make a step up into the cab. This arguably took another little part of the Bay's character away, but no one complained. Luxury Microbuses were offered with chromium-plated bumpers as an extra-cost option for the first time, while the other models had white painted ones, as usual. Bumper overriders were also extra-cost options by this stage, but gave the Bus a heavy, gawky appearance, and few outside the United States opted for them.

The VW roundel on the front panel – also chromed on luxury Microbuses – was reduced in diameter, and the front indicators were made square, and re-positioned above the headlamps on the outer ends of the fresh air-intake grille. This undoubtedly improved the frontal appearance of the Bus, but its practical value is difficult to appreciate.

The same applied to another change, in which the integral lock in the handle on the sliding door was made separate, and positioned on the door panel below the handle. This was so strange that Volkswagen owners began to suspect that the engineers and designers were running out of ideas.

An Automatic 'Box on Wheels'

In a courageous move, mostly with a view to the American market, Volkswagen decided to offer an automatic alternative. All 1.7-litre vehicles, except the Pick-Up, were offered with automatic transmission as an extra-cost option. A three-speeder with a conventional torque converter situated in the bellhousing of the gearbox, the automatic's ratios differed from the manuals and were as follows: first 2.65:1, second 1.59:1, third 1:1, reverse 4.45:1.

Back in 1968, both the Beetle and the Porsche 911 had been offered with semi-automatic gearboxes, the 911 being dubbed the 'Sportomatic'. Although the clutch pedal was done away with, changing gear still required the shifter to be moved, with the cog-swapping taken care of by electronics. No one really took to the semi-automatic Beetle, because the system sapped too much engine power and used too much fuel. And, once the late Denis Jenkinson had denounced the 911 in *Motor Sport* magazine, for being too far removed from Porsche's sporting image, the Stuttgart concern was also on to a loser. (Porsche did go on to develop its automatic PDK system for the Group C 962 racing cars, and its Tiptronic system for the production road cars with great success.)

In the 1970s, a Volkswagen with an automatic gearbox – even a fully automatic one – was not necessarily to be trusted. There was a mixed reaction. The British were sceptical about the potential lack of reliability, and

(Above) *Classic Splittie Transporters are now highly prized and sought after the world over.*

Devons were among the most popular of the British Camper conversions. Early examples like this are now extremely rare.

(Left) *Rumoured to have been styled along the lines of a Messerschmitt aeroplane, the old fashioned 'split' windscreen lasted until 1967.*

(Above, right) *The cab's interior was spartan and austere, but the high driving position gave a commanding view of the road ahead.*

(Above) *Heavy duty American-spec bumpers and sealed-beam headlamps are a strong styling feature, which improve the Splittie's aesthetics.*

With a much higher level of trim and roof 'skylights', the de luxe Microbus, or Samba, is the most coveted today.

(Above) *Standard or customized, the smiling 'face' always sits happily at the front of the 'box on wheels'.*

Despite fierce criticism of the Bus's handling from some quarters, a well-restored Splittie will still show a clean pair of heels to its peers, and a good many saloons.

(Below) *Opening 'Safari' windscreens and side doors provide just two ways of staying, and looking, cool in a customized Bus in hot weather.*

A '64 Panelvan makes for an ideal towing vehicle in the Santa Pod paddock.

(Below) *Top concours Sambas in these classic dual-tone colours, command 'big bucks' on both sides of the Atlantic and in Japan.*

(Bottom) *Although the Bay-Window models lacked some of the Splittie's character, they were a whole lot better on the road.*

With so much extra space in the Bay's 'living room', the specialist Camper converters had a field day.

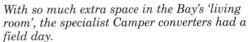

By the 1970s, Bay-Window Transporters had become a real alternative to 'middle-class' executive saloons like the Rover 2000 and BMW 2002.

(Above) *Renowned for its reliability and longevity, production of the classic, air-cooled flat-four powerplant, spans more than half the twentieth century.*

After the Samba, the double-cab Pick-up – Splittie or Bay, stock or custom – is the most popular model among young 'Volksheads'.

(Above) *Radically lowered, denuded of bright trim and with a 'permanently open' sunroof, this Cal-look Bay, despite its age, perfectly complements the modern building behind it.*

Although Volkswagen never made an official Camper version, demand for fully-kitted Bays continues to increase.

(Top) *Aerodynamically profiled fibreglass roofs overtook the elevating type in popularity during the 1980s, and also make the Bus more stable in crosswinds.*

(Above) *Even in its final 2-litre form, the Bay was deemed to be under-powered, but still capable of pulling over 80mph and returning reasonable fuel mileage.*

(Right) *Some 4ft longer than a standard Bus, the Dutch-built Kemperink was for those who wanted truck-like accommodation, but didn't want to leave the VW fold.*

The 'Wedge' was the last of the classic air-cooled Transporters. A much bigger vehicle, it was among the first commercials to put aerodynamic theory into practice.

(Below) *More sophisticated, roomier, safer, and unmistakably a Volkswagen, Wedge production ended in 1982 to make room for a new breed of water-cooled vehicles.*

the inherent complexities of the new transmission, and preferred to stick with what they knew and trusted. European commercial operators soon discovered the advantages of having no clutch pedal, particularly in busy urban areas, while the Americans felt completely at home with these versions.

With the Bus, the loss of engine power was, surprisingly, negligible, and the overall performance remained similar to that of the manual version. In contrast to many British and European vehicles fitted with automatic transmission during the 1970s, which were characterized by 'clunky' up and down changes, the Volkswagen's was comparatively smooth. The owner of a Bus with a manual gearbox commented in *Popular Imported Cars* that the new automatic was a 'joy to drive after shifting our Bus for the past two years'. She added, 'I'd like to call it "The People's Lib Bus" for those men and women who prefer exercising only when they feel like it.'

Interestingly, neither fully automatic transmission nor the 1.7-litre engine ever found their way into the Beetle.

Since 1950, the Volkswagen had come a long way. From a crude box with skinny crossply tyres, a feeble 25bhp engine, a non-synchromesh gearbox, the 'dreaded' swing-axle suspension, and interesting brakes, it had been transformed into a sophisticated, comfortable and quick conveyance with almost unrivalled equipment levels. About the only things that had not changed were its general shape, size and versatility.

Political Events

During 1952, just ten Buses had been sold in the United States. In 1955, 2,000 units were sold in a single year. In 1973, world-wide sales had tumbled to 174,121 units, a heavy drop by comparison with the 246,177 sold the previous year.

An odd year for motor manufacturing,

1973 was played out against a background of turbulent political events. In January, the Vietnam ceasefire agreement was signed, and in August American forces stopped their bombing campaign against Cambodia. But in October Egypt attacked Israel across the Suez Canal, and Syria attacked her on the Golan Heights. With the start of the Arab-Israeli war, Arab oil producers announced a cut in oil supplies, until Israel withdrew from occupied territories. As a direct result, fuel rationing was introduced in Britain and elsewhere, and many motor manufacturers were forced to focus on producing more fuel-efficient engines.

In fact, the war in the Middle East did not last long, and neither did fuel rationing, but these political events sent an important message to the motor industry.

A SIZE UP

While the oil crisis claimed a few notable victims in automobile manufacturing, Volkswagen replaced the short-lived 1700 engine with an improved 1800 unit. The replacement was to exactly the same design as the 1.7-litre, but with the cylinder bores increased in diameter from 90mm to 93mm to give a capacity of 1795cc (109.5cu in).

Despite the larger-diameter inlet and exhaust valves, power output rose to 68bhp, an increase of a paltry 2bhp, but there was an appreciable gain in torque, which went up from 81lb/ft at 3,200rpm to 92.4lb/ft at 3,000rpm. Top speed rose by a negligible 4mph (6.5km/h), to around 76mph (122km/h), and 60mph (96km/h) from rest took around 23 seconds. At a constant 60mph, fuel consumption had dropped to around 20mpg (14.15l/100km), but improved to 24mpg (11.8l/100km) at 50mph (80km/h). Many considered this to be a small price to pay for the gain in power, and completely acceptable in relation to the number of people or goods that could be carried. The fuel consumption figures were not, however, what had been expected after the restrictions imposed by fuel rationing.

THE MID-1970s

An Injection for America

The 1.8-litre vehicles exported to the United States were all fitted with Bosch fuel injection, in place of the more normal twin Solex carburettors. Those that were destined for California got a catalytic converter in addition, in response to the increas-

ingly serious problem of smog, especially in the Los Angeles area.

The fuel-injection system reduced variations in fuel-charge volume, as a result of engine-load changes, incorrect valve settings, carbon deposits and variations in exhaust back pressure. The amount of fuel injected was dependent on the volume of incoming air and engine revolutions. Alternate opening of the contact breaker points triggered each injection pulse.

Warming of the inlet air was controlled by an air-valve sensor and two temperature sensors. The former also adjusted the volume of fuel needed during acceleration. One fuel-injector nozzle was used for each cylinder, but, although all four were primed simultaneously, only two cylinders received the

From August 1972, the front indicators were placed above the headlamps on the outer ends of the fresh-air grille.

Banned in Germany at the beginning of the 1960s for safety reasons, headlamp 'eyelids' became popular accessories in the 1970s.

fuel/air mixture instantly. The other two cylinders stored the fuel/air mixture in the inlet manifold until the exact point at which their inlet cycle began. A computer – the infamous little black box – automatically calculated the moment of injection, based on electronic signals carrying information on engine revs, throttle setting, and volume of air. With electronic signals from the distributor and inlet air sensor, the computer was able to fathom the exact quantity of fuel and air required by the cylinders in any situation. Pressure in the fuel lines was maintained at around 35psi by a diaphragm, while the vacuum in the inlet manifold changed fuel pressure according to engine load.

Despite its inevitable complexities, the fuel-injection system proved to be extremely reliable and durable, with many Buses completing huge mileages without any major trouble. Faults that developed in the system could be traced easily and quickly, by plugging a dealer's electronic analysis machine into the socket in the engine bay. For many, the only disadvantage of fuel injection was that it took DIY maintenance well outside the scope of the 'tinkerer'.

Owners went to some lengths to maintain their vehicles. One well-known story continues to do the rounds in Volkswagen circles. An Englishman bought a house for his retirement on the island of Cyprus. He owned a fuel-injected Volkswagen and, assuming that garages and workshops on the island would not have the experience or equipment necessary to keep his vehicle in tip-top condition, he replaced the fuel-injection equipment with conventional carburettors. What he actually found in Cyprus was a Volkswagen garage, staffed by young technicians and state-of-the-art equipment, capable of dealing only with fuel-injected engines.

In most respects, the 1800 models were marvels. Their top speed was nothing much, but the extra power answered the many critics who kept on about the need to change down a gear while ascending steep hills.

There were a couple of disadvantages. The 1800 power unit was heavier than the 1700 it replaced, because the cylinder walls had to be increased in thickness. Some journalists reported that on automatics the transmission tended to get very hot during performance testing. They claimed that this led the gearbox to change up a gear some 5mph (8km/h) earlier than it should have done under normal driving circumstances. For the majority, however, it was still the best Bus anywhere on the market.

Other Changes

By the mid-1970s, the luxury Microbus had acquired alloy 'waistline' moulding strips, a retracting step to ease entrance through the sliding side door, and an optional heated rear window element. Tinted window glass was available as an extra-cost option on both Kombis and Microbuses.

The entire range was fitted with halogen headlamp bulbs, and thicker front discs to cope with the extra performance from the bigger engine. From the middle of 1974, a shear bolt was built into the steering column, and designed to snap off in the event of a collision, moving the steering wheel away from the driver in the process. These small changes were all well and good, but it was becoming apparent from the growing list of accessories and extra-cost options that ideas really were running out.

Problems

Volkswagen announced uncomfortable losses of DM800 million in 1973. Having weathered the oil crisis, and in the process of preparing for reaction to the new range of front-drive, water-cooled saloons, they avoided making expensive modifications to the Bus for the 1975 model year. Above all, modifications were not strictly necessary.

Although the Transporter continued as the top seller in many markets, worldwide sales began to decline by the mid-1970s. Camping versions by Westfalia and independent converters were more diverse in their fixtures and fittings than ever, and just as popular, but there were clear signals that the Bay's days were numbered.

THE END IN SIGHT

A Front-drive Revolution?

By August 1975, Volkswagen's board of directors had a clear picture of the future. Beetle sales had slumped badly, but sales of the new Golf, Scirocco, Polo and Passat were spiralling upwards. The car-buying public was voting heavily in favour of Volkswagens powered by engines that were both economical and powerful. Many VW traditionalists argued that the front-drive, front-engined revolution was a 'blip' that would not last. Even Volkswagen's sales and marketing department predicted that there would be no market for a GTi version of the Golf. They were all completely wrong.

The traditional Volkswagen badge fitted to the tailgate was dropped in 1972 ...

The 2-Litre Lump

But there was life in the old Bus yet. For the 1976 model year, the 2-litre engine, which was also employed in the recently revived Porsche 912 model (the 911 body with the 4-cylinder engine), and in the VW-Porsche 914, was slotted into the Bus as an alternative to the faithful twin-port 1600.

The 2-litre was Volkswagen's largest-ever production air-cooled engine, and a really 'lusty' piece of engineering. (An experimental 2.2-litre unit was thought to be on the cards at this time, but never went into production.) In reality, the 2-litre lump was an 1800 taken out to 1970cc (120.2cu in), by having its bore and stroke increased to 84 × 71mm; in this guise, maximum power of 70bhp was developed at 4,200rpm.

Twin Solex carburettors were fitted for most markets, and fuel-injected versions went to North America, as before. The power increase over the 1800 engine was

... and the VW roundel on the front panel was made smaller.

comparatively small, but an eight per cent gain in torque gave the Bus much-improved hill-climbing ability once again. Top speed was up – the 2-litre made 80mph (130km/h) cruising easy, where it was legally permissible – and fuel consumption was down on that of the 1800s. The capacity of the fuel tank was also reduced, from 13 to 11 gallons (60 to 50 litres).

Once it was 'bedded in', the 2-litre Bus was actually capable of speeds approaching 100mph 160km/h), even with a full load on board. German owners, with their speed limit-free *Autobahns*, enjoyed the new engine to the full.

Changes in the transmission included the final-drive ratio, reduced from the 1800's 4.86:1 to 4.57:1, and revised ratios in the automatic gearbox. They were: first 2.55:1, second 1.45:1, third 1:1. At the same time, the clutch plate was increased in diameter from 200mm to 228mm to enable it to cope with the increase in engine power and torque, and the electrical 'kickdown' facility on automatics was changed for a mechanically operated device. The front brakes were also uprated with the ATE front discs being changed for Girling units which had thicker pads.

Press Response

Despite these important improvements, journalists were generally becoming less enthusiastic about the Transporter. At the beginning of Bay-Window production, their road-test reports had been full of superlatives. By the mid-1970s, the majority acknowledged the brilliance of the design, but began more and more to criticize the mechanical specification, which, despite the many modifications, was beginning to look decidedly out-dated.

South African publication *Car* tested the Microbus – dubbed 'Executive' in that market – in August 1976. The writer of the report was predictably enthusiastic about the luxury fittings and carpeting, the vehicle's ability to transport up to ten people in comfort, and its exceptional braking performance, but was less impressed with other aspects of the vehicle.

He commented that, although the 0–100km/h time of 21.4 seconds was the best ever recorded with a VW Bus,

> the bigger engine did not feel all that much stronger than the 1800. It was necessary to use plenty of revs to counter a tendency to stall with quick clutch engagement. Rather surprisingly, the 2000 showed no gain in maximum speed – probably because the bigger engine is less free revving and achieves only what it is geared for.

Further criticism was again levelled at the 185×14 radial tyres and engine noise, despite further insulation materials having been placed at strategic points around the body, and thicker floor carpeting. The report concluded with mixed sentiments, remarking,

> considering the growth in engine capacity and improvement in gearing, the actual point-to-point performance of the Microbus 2000 may be disappointing to some people. But it scores in ordinary road performance (such as in overtaking, or on hills) and has increased towing ability for a caravan or trailer.

When the 2-litre model was debuted in South Africa, a Volkswagen spokesman was on hand at a press conference to point out that sales of the Transporter range regularly reached, or exceeded, 1,000 units per month. This amazing figure put the Bus above some of South Africa's best-selling passenger saloons, and had been acknowledged in the *Car* road test report. The writer finally commented as follows: 'The Kombi well deserves this distinction; it is a very honest vehicle, tremendously versatile, and holds a very special place in the family-car field in the Republic.'

The American publication *PV4* tested the 2-litre Kombi in January 1979, and criticized the vehicle's tendency to wander when buffeted by sidewinds. The writer of the report also noted the clatter from the flat-four:

> Cruising on pavement at 55mph [88km/h], that happy 3,000rpm torque peak could be felt and heard throughout the whole vehicle. After a time, the engine buzz at cruise became oppressive. Some additional sound-proofing is required here.

Without the benefit of sound-damping water jackets around the cylinder barrels, the air-cooled engine was inherently noisy; this was a feature of the Volkswagen that had once endeared it to so many people. The engine was now being condemned by some, comparing unfavourably with the comparative quietness of Volkswagen's 'water-pumping' saloons.

Some saw fit to dispense with the VW emblem altogether.

While journalists continued to be impressed by the precise handling, accurate steering, ride comfort and general all-round ability of the Bus, some dropped subtle hints about the type of unit that might power future generations of the Bus – it was not likely to be air-cooled.

PV4 concluded its report on a positive note, however:

> The Volkswagen has grown up along with surfers, the war-protester flower children of the 1960s and the vanthusiasm of the 1970s. This vehicle, for many families, for numerous roamers of the outback, has become the favoured friend of the road.
>
> Remember those service station hangers-on of 1949? Well, none of them are laughing now – and a lot of them are driving Volkswagen Station Wagons without so much as a snicker. In 27 years of development and refinement, Volkswagen has had the last laugh.

Last Years of Production

During the last four or five years of production, the specification of the vehicles began to diversify significantly according to the market for which they were destined. Cloth upholstery, for example, became available in the Kombi in place of vinyl, but not everywhere.

Volkswagen had set up factories in many parts of the world, and the overall specification of vehicles built in these factories differed markedly from that of home-grown products. South African Kombis, Pick-Ups and Panelvans, for example, continued to be fitted with the domed hubcaps that had been replaced on German-built vehicles in 1970. The Kombi built in South Africa also had five side windows instead of three, and wrap-around rear windows, reminiscent of the Samba Split-Screen models produced

For 1973, the bumpers were made stronger, and the front one no longer had its ends flattened to make a cab step.

prior to 1964. German-built Buses had been available in two-tone colour schemes for many years, but South African-built vehicles were not similarly adorned until the 1977 model year. Nor did they get 185 × 14 radial tyres and additional sound insulation until that year. Buses produced in South America were equally diverse.

Moving Upmarket

In the late 1970s, Volkswagen's board made a decision to change the image of the company's products. Economists at Volkswagen and Porsche were adept at predicting swings between economic boom and recession, and Volkswagen was in the happy position of owning an umbrella large enough to weather the severest of storms. The Volkswagen board decided to take advantage of increased public

spending power in the developed world, and go further upmarket.

During 1977 and 1978, the Transporter basically remained virtually unchanged, but a metallic-silver 2-litre Microbus with plush velour upholstery was made available for 1978; this was as far removed from the basic 'box on wheels' philosophy as it was possible to get. South African *Car* magazine noted in its December 1978 road test,

> The well-loved Kombi holds a special place in family motoring in South Africa – though in its modern form it seems to be getting beyond the means of the ordinary salaried man; the price of the 1978 top model (the Executive Automatic) is nearing 9000 rand.

In the United States, the basic Kombi model cost just over $6,000 in 1979, rising to more than $10,000 for the specially kitted out camping versions.

PORSCHE AND POLITICS

Arguably, Volkswagen misjudged the potential for four-wheel drive leisure vehicles. In most respects, the Bay-Window was an ideal off-roader – the rear weight bias gave excellent traction and, with four-wheel drive, it would have had goat-like climbing ability in difficult conditions. Five prototypes produced in 1978 proved this potential, but internal politics were to intervene and prevent production versions reaching the showrooms.

For many years, Volkswagen and Porsche had collaborated on dozens of engineering projects. The Stuttgart concern had received commissions from Volkswagen to design and test components, as well as complete vehicles, almost since Porsche had come into being, in 1948.

As the two companies grew, there were inevitable tussles, with directors having

103

conflicting views about the future prosperity of each. In his autobiography *Cars Are My Life* (Patrick Stephens Ltd), Ferry Porsche wrote,

> In 1974 we investigated the possibility of converting the VW Passat to four-wheel drive. I considered how our project would look in five years time, as shown by the success currently being enjoyed by various four-wheel drive vehicles. As long as the Porsche family had the final word in the company – it withdrew in 1972 – we did not necessarily take any wrong turnings.

Converting the Passat to four-wheel drive would have been a simple matter of fitting a propshaft and rear axle. However, Dr Fuhrmann, who sat on Porsche's board of directors, reported that W.P. Schmidt of Volkswagen was not able to supply Passats to Stuttgart for conversion. During dinner at the Volkswagen factory some time later, Ferry Porsche expressed his regret about

the situation to Schmidt. No one was more surprised than Schmidt. Fuhrmann had never mentioned the project to him.

Neither a Passat nor a Bay-Window Bus was ever to be equipped with four-wheel drive. Volkswagen did make the Transporter with the Syncro 'part-time' four-wheel drive system, but not before 1980, by which time the Japanese had cornered a large part of this market. Volkswagen could only pick up the crumbs.

Volkswagen was not alone in dismissing four-wheel drive as an ephemeral fashion. Several professional commentators and journalists considered that the majority of the car-buying public did not need all-wheel drive. In his May 1978 Kombi road test for Australian publication *Overlander*, Tony Curtis commented as follows:

> When the all-engulfing 4WD tide ebbs – as it eventually must – many of us will breathe a collective sigh of relief. And in that pleasant downtime before the next Big

The lusty 2-litre engine was the end of the line for air-cooling and debuted in 1975. A 2.2-litre version was rumoured to be on the cards, but never materialized in production.

The top-of-the-range Microbus has bright 'waistline' trim and a chromed roundel on the front panel, but Volkswagen had run out of ideas for improvements by the mid-1970s, and said so in publicity literature.

Fad comes flooding in, we should be able to gather our senses and consider the realities of horses-for-courses and trucks-for-tracks.

Curtis cited a contest between a Volkswagen Kombi and a Nissan Patrol on a tricky 40-degree hill near the Wombeyan Caves in New South Wales. The Kombi reached the top after the Nissan driver gave up. As Curtis noted, 'given the Kombi's torque and power–weight ratio with the engine over the rear wheels, the achievement was not surprising.'

The majority of Transporter owners on the African Continent and elsewhere, for whom serious off-roading was a way of life, adapted their vehicles by fitting a winch above the front bumper for pulling out of tricky situations. But the market for four-wheel drive off-roaders had been established, and was growing, and Volkswagen had clearly missed the boat.

Ray Barker, writing in the Australian journal *Bushdriver*, pointed out in his 1979 report on the Bus, 'If they made a 4 × 4 version, there would be a queue from Sydney to Melbourne.' Ferry Porsche had known this, but it seems that the great man's opinion had been ignored.

REFLECTIONS OVER THE BAY

A multi-purpose vehicle in the true sense, the second-generation Transporter was a huge success by any standard, with sales totalling more than 2.4 million units. In combining the ability to carry nine or ten people and their luggage, or hefty cargo, to cruise easily at 60–80mph (5–130km/h), and to drive like a well-honed family saloon, it was without rival. Despite its appearance it was shorter than an average American or Australian sedan, returned better fuel-mileage figures, boasted an almost unbreakable suspension system – unsurpassed in strength to this day – and was propelled by an engine of enduring quality.

Developed and perfected over a twelve-year period, the Bay was as popular with VW enthusiasts at the end of production, in July 1979, as it was on its debut, in August 1967. In its final year, the Kombi carried a price tag of $10,000 in the US, or $2,000 more than a comparable Japanese vehicle, but second-

hand Buses were snapped up as quickly as ever, despite remarkably low depreciation. The Volkswagen might have been relatively expensive, but it was a quality product without rival, and many were prepared to pay for that quality.

Right from the beginning of Splittie production, in 1950, Volkswagen had never been in the habit of making extravagant claims for the Bus, Beetle, or any of its models. The company's advertising was always totally honest, often naïve, and sometimes extremely funny. To own a Volkswagen in this classic era was to belong to an international club. Owners waved and flashed their headlamps at each other when they met on the road, and many continue this old tradition today. The Bay was correct for the modern age in which it was made.

One of five four-wheel drive prototypes built during 1978; internal politics prevented a production version.

5 Third-Generation Transporters: The Wedge

WIDER, LONGER AND MORE AERODYNAMIC

The last of the classic German-built air-cooled Buses were made between 1979 and 1982. Larger, more functional and significantly different from its predecessors, the Wedge – despite many changes – was still unmistakably from a Volkswagen mould, but it was made to cater for the needs of a rapidly changing world.

Commercial operators were demanding larger vehicles, and if Volkswagen was unable to supply exactly the type of vehicle required, there were plenty of other manufacturers who could. A large box was still a

Introduced in 1979, the Wedge was bigger and more spacious; the range was as comprehensive as ever, and the body shape was the first serious attempt to devise an aerodynamically efficient box.

pre-requisite of the design – some things never change – but this box took account of contemporary drives in the motor industry to improve aerodynamic efficiency, for the purpose of achieving higher speeds and saving fuel.

With this in mind, the front panel was made more curved, and the panel above the fresh-air intake grille was sloped at a steep angle. The similarly curved and much larger windscreen was posted at the same, steep rake. With its circular headlamps, centrally positioned V-over-W roundel, and large, impact-absorbing bumper, its front still resembled, like that of its two predecessors, a human face. However, it was no longer happy or smiling; it had taken on a rather lean and hungry look, reflecting Western political and social life of the time.

Although the same height as the Bay-Window model, the Wedge was a massive 5in (12.5cm) wider and 2½in (6.25cm) longer. The cab doors were much longer, as was the sliding side door, and both hugely improved access to the interior. The large top-hinged tailgate – supported by a damper on each side – ran from the top to the bottom of the body, in Splittie barn-door style. The separate external engine lid was banished to the mists of time once and for all. The rear window was an impressive 92 per cent larger than the Bay's.

Access to the engine was through a removable panel in the rear luggage compartment. And the luggage area here was also usefully increased in volume by the simple expedient of lowering the luggage platform by a marked 5½in (14.25cm). This was achieved by modifying the engine's ancillaries, so that the cooling fan was, once again, bolted to the nose of the crankshaft, and items such as the coil, alternator, fuel pump, distributor and air filter were moved to the sides of the power unit.

The range was as comprehensive as before, comprising a Panelvan, Kombi,

Microbus, high-top Panelvan and single- and double-cab Pick-Ups. On its launch, in 1979, the whole range was exceptionally well received, not only because the vehicle looked well and had more interior space, but because the engineering quality was still of the highest order. Over in Stuttgart, Daimler-Benz were also screwing commercial vehicles together rather well, but their products cost more than the Volkswagen. Many considered the Volkswagen to represent exceptional value for money, and even to be superior.

OLD HABITS ...

Altogether more sophisticated than the first two generations of Buses, the Wedge was designed and conceived by the people who were responsible for the company's extensive range of passenger saloons – the Golf, Polo, Passat and Scirocco. In common with these cars, the new Bus lacked some of the character of those that had gone before, but it was efficient and safe, and handled well. Interestingly, though, the Transporter continued with its engine at the rear driving the rear wheels, whereas the saloon cars had exactly the opposite arrangement.

The designers argued, quite correctly, that the rear was the best position for the power unit in commercial vehicles, because of the real problems of a lack of traction in front-drive vehicles, especially in wet conditions. There was also the company's history to consider. Volkswagen's customers expected the engine to be tucked away at the back, and, although a change in position was necessary – desirable even – in the saloon range, no one in Hanover or Wolfsburg was brave enough to make such a bold step with the Transporter. Its cult status and traditional following would remain intact – for the following ten years, at any rate.

Volkswagen Transporter 1979–82

Specification
Body type   Unitary construction

Engine
Type   Air-cooled horizontally opposed 4-cylinder
Capacity   1970cc
Bore   94mm
Stroke   71mm
Compression ratio   7.4:1
Cylinders   Detachable cast-iron barrels
Cylinder heads   Light alloy with two valves per cylinder operated by a single
                              camshaft and pushrods
Fuel system   Twin Solex carburettors in most markets; Bosch fuel injection for
                              North American models
Maximum power   70bhp at 4,200rpm
Maximum torque   98.6lb/ft at 2,800rpm

Gears
Gearbox type   Synchromesh 4-speed manual or 3-speed automatic
Gear ratios manual   First 3.78:1, second 2.06:1, third 1.26:1, fourth 0.852:1,
                              reverse 3.28:1, final drive 4.57:1
Gear ratios auto   First 2.55:1, second 1.45:1, third 1:1, reverse 2.46:1,
                              final drive 4.09:1
Clutch   Single dry-plate

Suspension, brakes and steering
Front suspension   Independent by upper and lower wishbones, coil springs, telescopic
                              dampers and anti-roll bar
Rear suspension   Independent by trailing arms, coil springs and telescopic dampers
Brakes   Hydraulically operated, dual-circuit front discs and rear drums
Steering   Rack and pinion
Wheels   Pressed steel 5-bolt 5.5J × 14 with 185 × 14 radials

Dimensions
Overall length   15ft (457.5cm)
Overall width   5.9ft (180.4cm)
Overall height   6.4ft (195.4cm)
Wheelbase   96.9in (246cm)
Track   61.8in (157cm)
Fuel tank capacity   13.2 gallons (50 litres)
Minimum ground clearance 7.5in (19cm)

Performance
Top speed   80mph (128km/h)
0–60mph (0–97km/h)   18secs
Standing quarter mile   19secs
Fuel consumption   21mpg (13.5l/100km)

Modern in every way, the Wedge still looks fresh today. From behind the wheel, like the Bay, it felt car-like, despite the necessarily high seating position. It stopped, steered and handled as well, if not better than any of its peers, and, thanks to improved upholstery fabrics, was considerably more comfortable than the Bay-window.

With such a large glass area – the windscreen was 21 per cent bigger – all-round visibility was outstanding. Meaty 185 × 14 radial tyres were fitted as standard, and roadholding was exceptional. A Wedge could be thrown safely through corners at high speed, despite the misgivings some journalists still had about the rear weight bias. In reality, the vehicle possessed virtually neutral handling characteristics; traditional Volkswagen over-steer was a thing of the past, and, if dyed-in-the-wool Bus people had any criticism, it was for this very reason.

A NEW SUIT, AND UNDERWEAR TO MATCH

Exterior

Although built to a fresh body design, the Wedge was constructed in much the same manner as the Bay. The bodyshell was of unitary construction, welded directly to a chassis frame, which had two parallel box-section longitudinals running from front to rear. Crossmembers and outriggers were welded to these longitudinals, both to support and strengthen the structure. The majority of body panels, such as the doors and rear side pieces, were constructed in Volkswagen's usual manner – single skins clinched to an inner framework. The floor of the cargo area, cabin and panel over the engine was single-skinned, but corrugated for extra strength.

The Panelvan remained the staple of the range, favoured by tradespeople the world over. The lack of bright trim was a contemporary trend.

The top-of-the-range luxury Microbus was externally distinguishable by anodized bright trim around the windows.

Swage lines were used at 'waist' level to break up the body's slab-like appearance, and there was a further one that bisected the wheel arches and lower body. The horizontal engine-cooling louvres followed Bay-Window practice, being placed in a near-vertical stack behind the rear side windows, but were much larger than before. The fuel filler neck was below the right-hand cab door, behind the front wheel arch. This was because the fuel tank was mounted much further forward to behind the front axle line, which improved the Bus's weight distribution, particularly when the tank was full.

Another area in which the Bus had been improved was in the steps taken to protect the metalwork from corrosion. All welded seams were coated with a thick, rubberized substance, and wax was injected into the box-sections.

Safety

Safety features carried over from the Bay-Window included a 'crumple' zone in the floor of the cab, and a collapsible steering column. The new bodyshell was so strong that the Wedge regularly beat its rivals in official crash tests.

The respected body of the Allianz Centre for Technology GmbH undertakes research into automotive accident damage for the German insurance industry. One of its many functions is to discover the economic realities of repairing vehicles involved in accidents. Much of the Allianz Centre's work down the years has shown that, in head-on collisions, there is an overlap of 30–50 per cent of the front of vehicles on the driver's side.

In one famous test, a VW Wedge was compared against several similar vehicles from

Japanese manufacturers. Driven by a guided sledge running in a central rail, each vehicle was smashed into a concrete block at around 21mph (35km/h), with a dummy strapped into the driver's seat. Each crash test was filmed, using high-speed cameras, and injuries to the dummy and damage to the vehicle were measured by electronic sensors. Of all the vehicles, it was discovered that the only one that could be repaired economically afterwards was the Volkswagen. It also had the least body deformation, and was the only vehicle among the sample whose doors could be easily opened from the outside after the crash. Most encouraging of all perhaps was that the dummy in the Wedge sustained fewer and less serious injuries.

For years, critics have complained that Volkswagen's products cost as much, if not more than their Japanese counterparts, which are always much better equipped. It is perfectly true that this has often been the case, but Volkswagen, along with Mercedes-Benz, Porsche and BMW, have always concentrated their efforts on engineering integrity. Primary and secondary safety, concepts that evolved in the 1950s, have always been considered more important by German engineers than filling a vehicle with electrical toys.

The general conclusion from the Allianz Centre's testing was that the Volkswagen Wedge Transporter was among the safest commercial vehicles in the world, and equal in terms of safety to a well-made saloon car.

A CLEANER CUT?

On all models, except the luxury Microbus, body trim was minimal. Chromium-plated bright trim and anodized alloy mouldings were no longer fashionable, added unnecessary weight, and were generally considered by designers in the motor industry to be

History repeats itself: the huge tailgate was reminiscent of early Barndoor Splitties.

rather brash. Even the bumpers on the Wedge were painted black, along with the door handles and the wing mirrors. In addition, the window glass was embedded in rubber that was without bright trim. The vehicles looked all the better for this treatment. With large square amber-lensed indicators below the circular headlamps, and tall, stacked tail-lamps, the new Bus was aesthetically clean and uncluttered.

The range-topping Microbus L – the luxury model – was rather less so. It was instantly recognizable externally by its anodized alloy trim mouldings applied to the window rubbers, including the windscreen and rear window. Further strips were at 'waist' level, along the sides of the vehicle, around the fresh-air intake grille on the front panel, and there was a decorative strip on the outside of the windscreen pillars. The bumpers had brushed aluminium strips applied to their upper and lower surfaces, there was a wash/wipe facility for the rear window, and additional sound-proofing materials in the doors and tailgate. In comparison with the other models, the luxury Bus resembled a fortune-teller's tent, but a minority continued to regard bright trim as a desirable luxury. A steel sliding sunroof was an extra-cost option.

One particularly interesting change was the location of the spare wheel, which was re-sited under the cab floor in a cradle. This created additional interior space, but it was rather inconvenient, especially for people suffering with back problems, to have to crouch down to get the wheel out from under the front bumper. The reasoning of Volkswagen's designers was, however, that changing a wheel would always be inconvenient, no matter where the spare was located.

SPACE, COMFORT AND MORE FRESH AIR

Once again, the interior had been vastly improved, and brought up to date. About the only aspect of the interior design that distinguished the Wedge from contemporary saloons was its width, and the huge amount of space. The Kombi and Microbus were available as eight- or nine-seaters, and the backrests of each seat offered really good lateral support for the first time. The squabs were also shaped, to offer a degree of lateral support for the thighs.

All seats were fitted with safety belts, as demanded by the legislation of the majority of countries at this time. The traditional 'dogstooth' vinyl upholstery, which had characterized much of the Bay-Window era, was changed for smoother vinyl that was easier

to clean, and the interior panelling and head restraints (where fitted) were covered in the same material. Launched in 1982 at the end of production, the special Caravelle model had velour upholstery, and bulky seat armrests covered in the same material.

The headlining was in cream-coloured vinyl, and extended to cover the window pillars on the luxury Microbus. All other models had exposed painted pillars, following the usual Volkswagen practice. Hard-wearing rubber mats were applied to the floors of the cab and rear area of the Panelvan and the Kombi, while the Microbus had carpeting. The cargo bed of the Pick-Up had strips of hardwood attached, as on previous models.

Heating for the cabin was supplied by the exhaust heat exchangers – no change there – with the amount of heat generated being largely dependent on the speed at which the vehicle was driven. This was hardly satisfactory by the late 1970s, and was just one of many reasons why Volkswagen switched eventually to water-cooled engines. Moves were made on the Wedge to improve fresh-air ventilation of the cabin. Large vents were

Thanks to the compact engine and the lowering of the panel above it, the luggage space in the rear was cavernous.

113

placed on each side of the dashboard, and there were two similarly large ones on each side of the roof in the rear passenger area.

Much of the dashboard was constructed of plastic, to save weight, and covered in a non-reflective material, including the upper surface below the windscreen. The instruments – central speedometer, fuel combination gauge to the left, and clock to the right – were shrouded by a large, curved binnacle. There was a blanking plate for a radio – still an extra-cost option – in the centre of the dashboard, and a deep glovebox in front of the passenger.

The steering wheel was a typically large two-spoker made in hard plastic, with 'man-sized' fingergrips on the underside, and a central horn button emblazoned with the VW emblem. Both manual and automatic transmission versions had floor-mounted shifters, the former fitted with a spherical knob, the latter with a T-handle; both were necessarily

long. The manual stick was the normal floppy item that felt unbalanced, unpleasant and often unfortunate in use. The conversion to right-hand drive, for the benefit of the British market and a minority of other countries, was particularly admirable on the Wedge. Past criticism of the pedals focused around them being awkwardly offset towards the centre of the vehicle, a problem from which right-hand drive Splitties, Bays, Karmann Ghias and Beetles had always suffered. The majority of drivers became well used to this, some to such an extent that they found conventional vehicles rather awkward. With more space, the Wedge's pedals were better placed and most comfortable.

RECOILING FROM THE PAST

The most radical – and inevitable – departure from conventional Volkswagen thinking

The much larger glass area gave an airy, light feel to the interior; ventilation, heating and standards of comfort were also improved. This is the nine-seater Kombi.

The plush Caravelle version boasted luxurious velour upholstery, head restraints and armrests all round.

occurred in the suspension department. Patented by Professor Porsche in 1931, the famous torsion-bar springing had to go. It was certainly tough and durable, and gave excellent ride comfort, but it was expensive to manufacture. Housed in wide-diameter steel tubing, the bars also took up a great deal of space. By the late 1970s, almost all manufacturers, with a few notable exceptions, had switched to coil-sprung suspension. Volkswagen had hinted at what the Transporter range could expect at some stage in the future by equipping the saloon range with coil springs from 1974. Ever mindful of the constant need to keep production costs down, the company's financial advisers and accountants were as much responsible for the change as the engineers.

Built to what is now considered to be an entirely conventional design – although radical for a VW Bus – the front suspension was independent, by upper wishbones and lower control arms, coil springs, telescopic shock absorbers, radius rods and an anti-roll bar. Attached to the vehicle by rubber bushes and brackets, the upper wishbones had a spindle, and eccentric washers for adjusting the camber angle. On the outside of the wishbones, the steering knuckle was attached to the hubs by maintenance-free balljoints.

The lower suspension arm was also pivoted on a rubber bush, and attached to the steering knuckle by an adaptor and balljoint. The anti-roll bar was fitted to each of the track control arms, rather than the trailing arms, as on torsion-bar vehicles of

Embossed with the VW emblem at its centre, the two-spoke steering wheel, although comfortable to use, typically lacked style. The instrumentation was bang up-to-date and in keeping with the contemporary saloon range.

the past. Made in one piece, the hubs had the brake discs fitted on their inner surfaces.

Also fully independent, the rear suspension was by trailing arms, telescopic dampers and coil springs, with drive being taken from the differential – housed in the gearbox – to the wheels by slim drive-

shafts, which, as on the Bays, had a CV joint on both the inner and outer ends, protected by rubber gaiters. This system differed from the Bay's in that the trailing arms were massive, heavy pieces, attached to brackets on the underbody by bolts and rubber bushes.

Although the front dampers were housed inside the coil springs, the rear ones were bolted to part of the chassis frame at the top, trailing arms at the bottom, and set at an angle.

Sourced from Volkswagen's large parts bin, steering was by rack and pinion, which made for even more precise handling and, in conjunction with the new suspension set-up, had the beneficial effect of reducing the turning circle to 35ft (10.5m). The steering column itself was made in two pieces joined by a safety coupling, which, like the shear bolt of old, was designed to snap in the event of a frontal impact. Regrettably, there is evidence to show that it works well.

A FINAL AIRING

The air-cooled Wedges were also offered with a choice of two engines. There was the faithful 1600 twin-port or the more powerful 2-litre unit, both of which had given long service in the Bay-Windows. Considering the additional weight of the Wedge, the 1600 was wholly inappropriate. With this power unit, changing gear was a constant necessity and very wearing, whereas the 2-litre engine, which would allow the Bus to cruise at around 86mph (138km/h), was just about adequate by the standards of the day. Although smooth, willing and 'throaty' – a nice engine – it was not especially thrifty

This cut-away clearly shows the sturdy longitudinal chassis rails, indirect steering, gearbox position and compact engine.

with fuel (an increasingly valuable commodity) and had a limited future.

The days of the classic air-cooled engine were numbered, its position threatened principally by huge forward strides in diesel-engine technology. By the end of the 1970s, customers demanded both power and fuel economy, and the 2-litre could give neither, by comparison with conventional engines.

One final change to the 1600 was dictated by the floor of the rear luggage compartment, which had been lowered by 5in (12.5cm). The old slogger was also turned into a 'suitcase' engine, like its more powerful sister, with the cooling fan on the nose of the crankshaft, and ancillaries positioned lower on the sides of the unit.

Due to legislative demands around the world, the differences between carburettor and fuel-injection settings became more marked than ever before. As previously, all Buses exported to California were com-

pulsorily fitted with catalytic converters and fuel injection, whereas all 2-litre vehicles exported to the other states in the US made do with fuel injection without cats.

Transporters sold in Europe and Britain with 2-litre engines had twin Solex 34 PDSIT carburettors, while the 1600 received its fuel supply from a single Solex 34 PICT-4 carburettor. And, whereas both 1600s and 2-litres in Europe and most other markets had mechanical fuel pumps, the American-spec 2-litres had an electrical pump situated in series with the main fuel pipe from the tank under the vehicle.

Apart from the catalytic converters fitted to Californian Buses, exhaust emission controls were taken care of in two different ways. A closed-circuit crankcase ventilation system was used, allowing emissions from the crankcase to be re-circulated to the air cleaner. A breather pipe on the crankcase directed fumes to the air cleaner, where

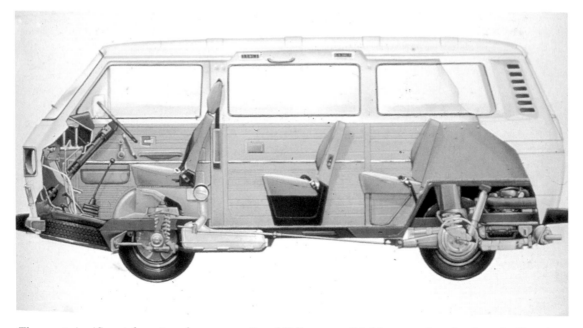

The most significant departure from conventional Volkswagen thinking was the adoption of coil-spring suspension instead of torsion bars. The spare wheel was also moved from the rear luggage area to below the cab floor.

they mixed with the fresh intake air and eventually got burned within the engine.

The other method was by the system of exhaust gas re-circulation, or EGR. This was used to minimize the amount of nitrogen oxide being produced during combustion. A small quantity of the exhaust gases was ducted back into the inlet manifold and mixed with the fuel/air mixture. An EGR valve controls exhaust-gas delivery to the manifold through a filter. This made the combustion process a lot cleaner, and actually reduced emissions of nitrogen oxide.

In a roundabout way, the emissions equipment put the final nail in the coffin for the air-cooled engines. Apart from being complex and expensive to repair when things went wrong, emissions equipment robbed the engine of much-needed power. To solve the problem, some manufacturers, including Porsche and Daimler-Benz, simply kept on increasing the cubic capacity of their engines. Volkswagen could not increase the size of the 2-litre motor without sacrificing reliability and increasing noise levels. To all intents and purposes, its development was over. Adding two more cylinders and a further 400cc would have been desirable from a driver's point of view, but doing this would have been prohibitively expensive, and would have incurred the wrath of Porsche.

Bus owners were given a choice between a paltry 50bhp with the 1600, or 70bhp with the 2-litre. Although to the same outdated design, these engines had been modified in three important ways. For the first time on a Volkswagen, hydraulic tappets were fitted, which did away with the tiresome task of manually adjusting conventional tappets, and also made for quieter running. Electron-

Access to the 2-litre 'suitcase' engine was through a removable hatch in the rear luggage compartment.

1. Transporter-Generation 1950 bis 1967

Im reichlich dimensionierten Motorraum mit luftgekühlter 1,1-Liter-Vierzylinder-Boxermaschine haben rechts das Reserverad und links der Kraftstofftank Platz.

2. Transporter-Generation 1967 bis 1979

Außer der Heckklappe für Wartungs- und Servicearbeiten ist der Motor von oben zur Durchführung von Reparaturarbeiten zugänglich. Zum 1,6-Liter-Boxer- mit stehendem Gebläse kommt 1971 ein 1,7-Liter-Flachmotor (Foto) hinzu. Er wird 1978 im Hubraum auf 2,0-Liter und in der Leistung auf 51 kW (70 PS) angehoben.

3. Transporter-Generation ab August 1979

Eine weitere Absenkung des Motorraums wird durch die konstruktive Vereinheitlichung der luftgekühlten Boxer-Motoren mit Kühlluftgebläse auf der Kurbelwelle möglich. Große Klappe über dem Motorraum, tägliche Kontrolle von hinten durch wegklappbare Kennzeichenbefestigung. Der seitlich geneigt eingebaute, wassergekühlte Reihen-Dieselmotor begnügt sich mit dem gleichen Platzangebot wie die luftgekühlten Boxer-Triebwerke.

ic ignition was fitted, to ensure that the engine stayed in tune longer, and there was also a micro-computer, used to control slow running. Dubbed 'Digital Idling Stabilization', the computer system helped to stabilize the fuel/air mixture more carefully, so that the age-old problem of the engine cutting out on cold mornings or proving reluctant to start when hot, was eliminated almost overnight.

At a Silverstone test day in 1980, where assorted sports cars from various manufacturers were made available for journalists to try, Robin Wager of *Safer Motoring* magazine had the chance to test a 2-litre Panelvan around the Grand Prix circuit. He wrote,

> Now for something completely different – and I was the only person at the event who took out the new VW Transporter. Hardly the vehicle for the GP circuit, you may think, but I overtook a surprising number of cars in this splendid carry-all, the only air-cooled survivor in the range.
>
> This 2-litre version (like its 1600 alternative) has more or less the old engine, made a little more compact for a lower floor; but everything else about it is new, from the all-round coil spring suspension to the Golf/ Polo derived instrument panel. The gear lever looks as if someone has leant on it until you find it really is meant to be bent towards the driver at that angle!
>
> The old characteristics are still in the engine, which will rev happily (I saw 70mph |112km/h| in third) and helped me to take advantage of the van's new-found cornering power (there were some surprised faces in quite respectable saloons as the VW swept through on the outside of the bends!).'

A contemporary Volkswagen advertisement shows remarkable engine development, from the prototype through three generations. Despite appearances, the basic design of the air-cooled flat-four was fundamentally unchanged.

Robin Wager had always been an enthusiastic driver, particularly of Volkswagens, but his impressions were similar to those of most journalists and owners. However, although the vehicle really could be slung around in safety, so could other commercial vehicles. Volkswagen could not afford to lose their competitive edge, and they had to find something extra to put one over on the competition.

THE BOX BETWEEN THE WHEELS

The 4-speed synchromesh gearbox, with its ribbed alloy casing, was to Volkswagen's traditional design, and bolted to and in front of the engine. A single dry-plate clutch was common to all manual transmission models, and was located in the bellhousing at the rear of the gearbox. Vehicles supplied with the 1600 engine had a 215mm-diameter clutch operated by cable, whereas 2-litre versions had a hydraulically operated 228mm-diameter unit.

The clutch-release mechanism was the same on both types, and comprised a release shaft and bearing situated in the bellhousing at the rear of the gearbox. Both models shared the same ratios on the first three gears and were as follows: first 3.78:1, second 2.06:1, third 1.26:1. Top gear differed, with a ratio of 0.823:1 (0.852:1 in some markets) in the 1600, and 3.28:1 in the 2-litre. At 3.28:1, reverse was the same on both, whereas the final-drive ratio on the 1600 was 5.43:1 (or 5.86:1), and 4.57:1 on the more powerful of the two vehicles.

As 'bullet-proof' as ever, the gearbox was still good for many thousands of miles of use and abuse, and remained as an outstanding tribute to Volkswagen's faith in developing tried and tested principles laid down by Professor Porsche many years earlier.

With vastly increased access to the cabin and improved interior space, the independent Camper converters once again had a field day.

Automatic versions were also to virtually the same design as before, and comprised a torque converter instead of a conventional clutch, the epicyclic geartrain and final-drive assembly. The gear ratios were: first 2.55:1, second 1.45:1, third 1:1, reverse 2.46:1, and 4.09:1 for the final drive.

The performance of the automatic gearbox was typical of those from European manufacturers of this period; up and down changes were slightly 'clunky', and the units could sometimes (although not always) be unreliable. The Americans clearly led the rest of the automotive world in this area of engineering.

The Americans enthused more about the automatic Buses than the British and Europeans did. Interestingly, the long-standing editor of *Motor Sport*, Billy Boddy, who once wrote a regular column for *Safer Motoring* magazine, commented in 1979,

There's no longer any shame in admitting that you actually prefer an automatic gearbox. It seems to me that at last automatic transmission is becoming acceptable, even to the keenest drivers – except for a few diehards from the old school ... who think that if you cannot swap cogs without crashing 'em, you are not a motorist.

How times change!

STOPPING POWER

To cope with the Wedge's extra weight, the braking system was upgraded, but entirely conventional in every way. Dual-circuit hydraulics were used, with 278mm-diameter discs and Girling or Teves double-piston fixed calipers at the front, and 252mm-diameter single leading shoe drums at the rear. A servo was fitted to all 2-litre versions, but not to the 1600.

As with the Bays, the dual-circuit layout was split front to rear, with the primary circuit operating on the front brakes, and the secondary one on the rear. A pressure regulator in the rear system reduced the potential for the rear wheels to lock up under heavy braking. The regulator worked and formed the primitive beginnings of today's ABS systems.

Brake cooling was aided by the same five-bolt 5.5 × 14 perforated wheels that were fitted to the Bay-Window models.

PEN POWER

Doyen of the Volkswagen Camper world, Chris Burlace, for many years of *Safer Motoring* (later *VW Motoring*) magazine, with thousands of pages of copy on all things VW Bus to his name, approved wholeheartedly of the new models. When he tested a Devon Moonraker conversion in May 1980, he criticized Volkswagen for taking so long in getting a right-hand drive version ready for Britain, but admitted that the long wait had been worthwhile.

By this time, Chris Burlace was one of the few journalists who drove test vehicles for hundreds of miles, to discover what they were really like, before bashing out his views on a typewriter. On a long trip to Derbyshire and back in the Moonraker, he recorded an average of 24mpg (11.8l/100km) from the 2-litre engine, and found driving the Wedge a delight.

Cab comfort is up to passenger-car standards, with the brushed nylon upholstered seats fitted with headrests in the Moonraker, adjustable for reach and rake. The driving position of the older Volkswagen commercials was always good, but the new van represents a significant advance in this respect. The revised steering wheel angle sets it ideally for a comfortable ten-to-two grasp and everything is to hand. The gear change is more positive, with shorter travel between positions and, a pointer to revisions in the gearbox itself, reverse gear is now alongside first instead of second.

He went on to praise the floor-mounted handbrake lever, 'a great improvement' over the Bay's umbrella affair, and the layout of all switchgear. Most telling of all was Burlace's insistence that the ride quality was 'in the limousine bracket'. He remarked,

Whether in the cab or riding on the correctly contoured rear bench seat, where the extra width of the VW has been employed to improve seating and sleeping space, comfort was assured. Some vans can provide an equal or marginally better ride in the front, over good roads, but none can match the Volkswagen when the going gets rougher and none will provide a better ride over any type of surface than the Moonraker gives its rear seat occupants.

Safer Motoring was clearly giving the thumbs up to the new coil-spring suspension system, of which some Volkswagen folk

The last of the classic air-cooled Buses rolled out of Hanover in 1982, but enthusiasts continue to enjoy them for their intended purpose.

123

had at first been highly sceptical. In fact, all the journalists who drove the vehicles were impressed by them, and agreed that they were hugely improved.

THE END OF THE WEDGE?

Persistent rumours that water-cooled engines were on the way, as a replacement for the traditional air-cooled units, shook a hardcore of Volkswagen aficionados. To some, a water-cooled Volkswagen was not a 'proper' Volkswagen, and many refused to believe that the people in Hanover and Wolfsburg could think of such a concept for the Bus.

However, they had, and this was why the air-cooled Wedge remained the same at the end of production as it had been at the beginning. It is perhaps telling that *Safer Motoring*, Britain's only magazine at that time which regularly devoted space to air-cooled Volkswagens, gave so little coverage to the Wedge.

The little copy that was published talked almost exclusively about luxurious camping conversions, and there was a clear message from the writers of these reports. Volkswagen Campers were market leaders, but the cost of such luxury was spiralling upwards. In short, Volkswagens were quickly becoming beyond the financial reach of their traditional customers. Even as late as 1981 – two and three years after production of the Bay-Window had ceased – some specialist camping converters were offering refurbished second-hand Bays for sale. They found a ready market, for the simple reason that the Wedges were too expensive.

The air-cooled Wedges were replaced in 1982 by diesel-powered and water-cooled petrol engines, which were more economical and powerful. The same body style was retained, but the later vehicles can now be distinguished by the horizontal radiator grille on the front panel.

6 The Campers

CARAVANS AND CARAVANNING

Between the two world wars, the traditional caravan was an ungainly, coach-built mobile home that was generally out of the financial reach of ordinary working men and women. Even for those 'ordinary' people who could afford to buy and run a car, owning a caravan was out of the question, as most cars did not have sufficient engine power to tow one. Caravan use was the exclusive privilege of the well-heeled who could afford the expensive car needed to pull it.

After the end of the Second World War, manufacturers continued to produce caravans, in comparatively small numbers, for the same clientele. Traditional craftsmen were employed to produce ornate interiors, often in expensive hardwoods. The cupboards bulged with the best bone-china teasets, there were brass candleholders screwed to the walls, and the finest quality

A fully mobile home in secluded countryside; the Volkswagen Camper provided a perfect means of escape.

Westfalia, officially appointed converters, maintained high standards, but were conservative in their approach to elevating roof design, as this early publicity shot illustrates.

carpeting lay on the floorboards. In Britain, you might see a TA14 Alvis towing one of these monstrosities, boiling its radiator, crawling up steep inclines; it was a sight that often signalled the beginning of a frustrating holiday on the road for the occupants of the Alvis.

Today, the powerful motor cars needed to pull caravans are widely available, and caravanning is more popular than ever. Back in the early 1950s, Westfalia was the first company to spot in the Volkswagen Transporter an affordable alternative to the cumbersome car-and-caravan combination.

WESTFALIA

Beginnings

Founded in 1844 by Johann Knobel, the Westfalia company was originally concerned with the manufacture of agricultural tools and implements, swiftly gaining a foothold in the market for horse-drawn carriages by 1850. Employing some of Germany's finest craftsmen, the firm established a reputation for outstanding quality, and for never faltering in its standards. Westfalia's coaches were by no means the cheapest products available, but they were among the best and most dependable. A paint and upholstery shop had been set up by 1887, in keeping with Knobel's long-held ambition to become a wholly independent manufacturer, without having to rely on supplies and help from outside.

By the 1930s, Westfalia had also joined the ranks of caravan and camping trailer manufacturers, but they were producing the heavy pieces that could only appeal to those with enough money to stretch to a multi-cylinder Horch, Wanderer or Mercedes-Benz too.

In common with so many German companies, Westfalia saw its factories badly damaged by Allied bombing raids during the war; its plant at Sandberg was completely reduced to rubble. It was the same story for Volkswagen at Wolfsburg. The only route to a successful economic future for either of these great companies was to make the best of the tools and equipment that remained, and start the long process of re-building. By 1947, Westfalia had recovered sufficiently to exhibit their first steel-plate caravan at the Hanover Fair. Lacking the grandeur and glamour of today's motor shows, with the German economy in a poor state, Hanover welcomed few visitors in 1947. For Westfalia, however, there was a

In Britain, the Devon Caravette name became synonymous with VW Campers.

A hardworking Devon motor caravan earns its holidays in the sun

An early Devon brochure seeks to demonstrate the versatility of one of their vehicles – a workhorse during the week that quickly converts to a holiday home.

bright light at the end of the tunnel, in the form of the VW Transporter.

The First 'Campmobile'

When the Transporter was launched officially, in 1950, the people at Westfalia, who had rarely been slow to capitalize on new markets in the past, immediately recognized the potential for a wholly new type of camping machine. In the Transporter Westfalia saw not only a new camping vehicle, but a new camping concept – an affordable alternative to the trailer caravan – which would open up new ways of life and motoring for thousands of people wishing to make more of the small amount of leisure time they had. A self-propelled, self-contained motorized caravan appeared to make sense for a country that was beginning to recover from the ravages of the time of 'Herr Hitler' (as Professor Porsche had always addressed him). In 1951, Westfalia launched the first 'Campmobile'.

To begin with, production was necessarily slow – it took until 1959 for the 1,000th vehicle to be completed – but for those who saw the fully kitted Camper as a means of escaping from the humdrum of their over-worked daily lives, the Volkswagen Camp-mobile was a godsend.

The interior of the early Westfalias was deceptively simple. A large wooden cupboard was attached to the inside of one of the opening side doors for storing cutlery and gro-ceries, and there was also a small but conve-nient washbasin here. Curtains were provided for each of the non-cab windows.

A folding table and chair sat in the centre of the rear passenger area, with a folding bench beside it on one side, and another bench on the other. A full-width bench seat was placed at the rear of the vehicle, along with a storage cupboard. A small camping stove and icebox were also part of the package.

Converting this comfortable sitting room into a bedroom was an easy matter of folding away the central table, and rolling the bench seats over to produce a couple of double beds. There was a handy locker at the rear for hanging clothes, and ample space beneath the beds for suitcases. An awning and poles were stowed away below the rear bench seat; this could be erected on the outside of the two side doors in a matter of minutes. Made of plastic, it provided a useful 'storm' porch, or somewhere to sit out of the wind.

Many converters offered an awning of some description; this 'storm' porch provided basic cover against the elements.

A full-sized tent for the side of the vehicle came at extra cost, but it doubled the useful living or sleeping space.

Freedom and Versatility

Above everything, the Campmobile offered people the freedom they craved. As the writer of *Motor Trend*'s report in October 1956 remarked,

> If you don't want to be dependent on motels, if you like to stop for a day or a week where the trout are biting or the view is straight out of a travel folder, look out! This homely vehicle could make you quit your job, sell your house, or otherwise lose control.

It soon became apparent that owning a Camper was an ideal means of escaping, and the vehicle also doubled as a reliable, low-cost daily hack during the working week. No seat belts were fitted and other safety features were almost non-existent, but none of these considerations mattered to Camper devotees.

By 1971, Westfalia had produced 100,000 Campmobiles, and were knocking out 100 units per day. Many people were discovering that the Westfalia had a great many more uses than as a camping vehicle. Business people delighted in the advantages of a mobile office, fishermen found a motorized lodge, mothers had a convenient children's changing room, and racing drivers discovered a peaceful refuge in between qualifying sessions. Car devotees rather looked down on the Camper in the metaphorical sense, while Camper owners quite literally looked down on car drivers; those car drivers who converted to a Camper rarely looked back.

129

The only major drawback, which afflicted the vast majority of Camper conversions down the years, was condensation on the windows and walls in certain weather conditions. Some found this so intolerable that, after their first soaking, they sold their vehicle, never to return to the fold. These people were few and far between; the majority were always prepared to trade minor discomforts for the many advantages.

INDEPENDENT CONVERTERS

Westfalia clearly established itself as a leader in this fledgling market. Such was the high quality of the fixtures and fittings in the Campmobile that the tables, chairs and cupboards lasted for years, and re-sale values were always high. However, this sort of quality was relatively expensive – Westfalia vehicles were never cheap to buy new – and this prompted many VW folk to buy Panelvans or Kombis, and do their own conversions.

Panelvan owners cut apertures into the sides of the bodywork, installed window glass, and kitted out the interior to their own specification. Some conversions were to a very high standard, with the art of the cabinet-maker being employed to the full in some cases, while others were downright crude.

In Germany and North America, the officially sanctioned Westfalia conversion was by far the most popular, despite the relatively high purchase price, but in other parts of the world there were dozens of independent

A roll-top sunroof solved the perennial headroom problem in fine weather, but ...

manufacturers. Each of these companies had their own ideas about best utilizing the Bus's interior space. The majority of them operated by purchasing new vehicles from Volkswagen – mostly Kombis – and then carrying out the conversion work on their own premises. Some converters, however, offered special designs for private customers, catering for individual needs. As a result, there are no hard and fast rules as to the specification of each model.

Apart from the special, large-bodied vehicles that could sleep up to nine people, the majority of Campers were designed to cater for two adults and two children. A second category designed to sleep two adults was generally better equipped, while a third type catered for both camping and load-carrying.

THE BRITISH CONVERTERS

Dozens of different designs appeared, based on the broad themes, and the British were among the best. At the time when the first right-hand drive Buses arrived in Britain, in 1953, there was still a strong anti-German feeling. Many early Beetle imports were vandalized, and in some quarters the idea that the Bus and Beetle were part of Hitler's policy of post-war revenge was perpetrated well into the 1960s.

The Devon Range

The more enlightened really took the Camper to their heart. Lisburne Garage of

... a Martin Walter side-elevating roof was a better solution.

Some converters favoured large, boxy roofs, not only for their generous headroom, but because they were more easily fitted with children's bunks.

Babbacombe Road, Torquay, was one of the first to realize the potential for profit, and had launched the famous Devon range of Campers by 1957. The old established cabinet-making firm of J.P. White, based in Sidmouth, carried out the interior joinery work to such a formidably high standard that many original examples of their craftsmanship remain in good order today.

Based on the Microbus, Devons were available in three levels of 'trim' and, from top to bottom, were the Torvette, Caravette and Devonette. In 1958, the Caravette, which was to prove the most popular for many years, cost a reasonable £897, and provided holiday accommodation for two adults and as many children. With the camping equipment removed – not a difficult job – it could easily be converted back to its original function of carrying up to eight

people by the simple installation of the original seats.

The Caravette did not have the range-topping Torvette's double rear cupboard, but its equipment level was nevertheless very good. There was a double bed-cum-dinette in the centre, two formica-covered tables – one sliding, one folding – storage cupboards and a locker. A twin-burner gas cooker was cleverly built into the one of the cupboards.

Early vehicles were without washing facilities, but water tanks and basins were provided by 1958. Curtains were featured all round. Additional interior lighting was run directly from the battery, which sometimes proved to be something of a problem. With pre-1966 6-volters, the battery could run perilously short of power if the interior lighting was on for several hours, and this is why the Caravette was also provided with gas lighting, run from a Calor cylinder stored in a locker below the transverse bed at the rear. For safety reasons, the cylinder was coupled to an external point when being used.

A fire extinguisher was not generally provided by manufacturers in the early days but, after a minority of owners discovered to their cost that a Camper would burn out in a matter of minutes if the event of a fire, this vital piece of equipment became part of the overall specification.

Without the benefit of an extending or elevating roof, headroom was limited, particularly for cooking. Many manufacturers got around this problem by offering large tents (at extra cost) that fitted to the sides of the bodywork. These not only provided a place in which to cook, but gave an extra sitting room or bedroom.

By 1958, the purchase price of a Devon Caravette had risen to £930, but the increase was justified by improved trim and equipment levels. *The Motor* tested one in November of this year, and remarked,

Motor caravans as a species have merits and demerits in relation to the trailer-type caravans, which are quite straightforward: given that only limited accommodation is needed, a self-propelled caravan is faster, more manoeuvrable, probably more economical and can be parked on any site which will accept a car: moreover the Caravette restarted on a 1-in-3 gradient.

These were clear advantages, but the writer of the test report added,

On the debit side, it is less comfortable to sit in or drive than the family car which would ordinarily be used as a tug, and the caravan part necessarily accompanies the driver like Mary's little lamb, whether it is wanted or not. A typical trailer caravan motorist might have a maximum speed of 75mph

The children's bunks were side-by-side, fold-away items and gave even quite large youngsters a surprising amount of room.

[120km/h] with the caravan left at home, or 30mph (legal) [48km/h] maximum when towing, whereas the motor caravanner has 60mph [96km/h] available every day.

As ever, you pays your money …

Impartial critics of the Volkswagen Camper failed to take into account the fact that this type of vehicle always meant more to its owner than a means of transport and a convenient mobile home. By the beginning of the 1960s, it had come to represent a seriously 'light-hearted' way of life.

As time went on, the Devons became better-equipped, as competition from other manufacturers and VW specialists became intense. They also increased dramatically in price, especially when fitted with a Martin Walter side-elevating roof. By the mid-1960s, the cost of the top model was well in excess of £1,000, or roughly £400 more than the de luxe 1200 Beetle.

The Slumberwagen

In London's South Kensington, European Cars Ltd produced their Slumberwagen version on the camper theme (also based on the Microbus). This had a most unusual Calthorpe elevating roof, giving the Bus something of the look of a pre-war trailer caravan. It was not especially good-looking, but interior headroom was first class. The side pieces of this roof also incorporated sliding windows, for improved ventilation. The writer of *The Autocar*'s test on this model, in April 1960, concluded,

> This weekend journey in the Microbus left the firm impression that from the driver's point of view on long journeys it's one of the best motorized caravans. The caravan conversion makes no pretence to house more than two adults and two children, but this accommodation is provided efficiently, and makes good use of the space available. The construction of the fittings sets a high standard, and careful thought has gone into the design of the conversion.

With the stove fitted to one of the side doors, it was possible to cook outside or inside the vehicle.

The Autohome

By the early 1960s, Leeds-based Moortown had joined the race to produce a VW Camper; like so many other conversions, their Autohome model was based on the Microbus. This was not the cheapest conversion, but it was a good one, catering for two adults and two children for sleeping purposes, or up to six people in 'non-sleeping' mode. Again, early examples were without an elevating roof, so dressing and undressing with the beds laid out was problematic, especially for tall people.

As in the Slumberwagen, there was a bunkbed arrangement in the cab, where the backrest of the bench seat was used as the upper bunk, and the squab for the lower one. Partition panels were provided, which could be hooked up to prevent a child from rolling out of bed. The main double bed in the centre of the vehicle was made up by folding over the main bench seats; the dinette-type table could also be folded away, and stored in a panelled compartment behind the driver's seat – a neat arrangement.

The perennial problem of finding a safe yet convenient location for cooking was solved by placing the two-burner gas plate in a cabinet attached to the side door, with the gas bottle immediately below it. This thoughtful arrangement allowed the cooker to be used both inside and outside the vehicle. A locker on the other side door housed a wash bowl, and a push-pull pump for drawing water from the tank below.

All the specialist converters worked within the same confines – few made bodywork modifications to create additional space – but Moortown proved to be particularly adept at making the most of what was available. Shelved cupboards were built into the space above the engine, leaving a generous amount of room for luggage. In addition, there was a good-sized wardrobe, racks for cutlery and crockery, lockers below the

Bespoke wood panelling was not uncommon, and several converters employed the best craftsmen to produce sumptuous interiors; this standard of fitting was far from cheap, however.

Many individual owners had their own ideas for interior layout. This home-made job uses modern fabrics and a rear seat, which, in conjunction with the luggage space above the engine, easily converts to a large double bed.

This customized Bus retains the original wood cabinet on the side door, and blanket box beneath the rear-facing bench seat.

seats for storing bedding, and a small cupboard for storing shoes.

After carrying out extensive tests in 1961, *The Motor*'s reporter found nothing worthy of criticism other than the cooker. This item was condemned for a particular reason:

For most purposes, this device worked very well, but our addiction to morning toast remained unsatisfied because no griller is fitted. This absence also raises plate-warming problems, which were ultimately solved by first using them as saucepan lids.

(Warming the plates on a camping expedition was presumably considered more important forty years ago than it is today!)

Modifications and Performance

Despite the extra weight of the camping equipment, the performance of these vehicles was just about adequate by contemporary standards. *The Motor*'s data on the Moortown Autohome was typical of the majority of conversions. Top speed with the 34bhp 1200cc vehicles was around 60mph (96km/h), 0–40mph took 17 seconds, and fuel consumption typically averaged out at around an impressive 25mpg (11.3l/100km).

The report concluded,

The usual good finish of VW products is matched by the quality of the interior furnishings and fittings so, while the Autohome, as tested, costs £982, and is by no means the lowest-priced conversion available, even from Moortown, it will undoubtedly inspire pride of possession in those who care to pay that little extra.

By 1962, the Devon range, and the Caravette in particular, was better-equipped than ever, and consequently put on weight. In de luxe Microbus guise, and fitted with a Gentlux elevating roof, the purchase price had increased to £1,185, closer to the cost of a luxury saloon car.

Modifications to the interior included a sink at the rear of the vehicle, to the left of the bench seat. This had a much more satisfactory water pump, fitted with a rocking handle in place of the previous push-pull mechanism. The fold-away cooker was attached to the cupboard behind the front cab passenger. The gas bottle used to power the cooker was hidden away in the engine compartment, and had a rubber pipe for

Although Splittie Campers are much coveted today, owners continue to use them with undisguised enthusiasm for their original purpose.

Reformed drug addict, Ian Flynn, from Liverpool, has proved that it really is possible to live in a Camper, having done so for more than ten years.

connection to a gas point externally. An Easicool food and drink storage box was standard. Many different types of side awning were available at extra cost, either as the closed-in tent type, or the simpler flat-roof variety, with collapsible metal poles and support ropes. A toilet tent was also available at extra-cost, and proved surprisingly popular.

Despite the Caravette's extra weight, as *The Autocar*'s testers made clear in their 1962 report, performance had not suffered. Even though journalists did not have sophisticated timing equipment, and allowing for a small margin of error, the performance figures seem to have been broadly accurate, and were confirmed by owners time and again. *The Autocar* recorded a best top speed of 63mph (100km/h), 0–40mph from rest in 17 seconds, and overall fuel consumption of

23.1mpg (12.25l/100km). Again, these were remarkable figures considering the vehicle's paltry 34bhp, and comparatively dismal aerodynamic qualities.

With the weight of the camping gear confined to the area between the front and rear axles, Campers handled as well, if not better than, for example, an unladen Panelvan. However, this attribute of the Camper was not recognized by all motoring journalists. Some, like those on *The Autocar*, made negative assumptions about the handling, based on the rear position of the engine and gearbox, without testing the vehicle properly. The writer of the 1962 report remarked that:

> Marked over-steer results from the rearward weight distribution, though at 24cwt, the Caravette is one of the lighter motorized caravans. This tail-heaviness may also play some part in the pronounced effect which sidewinds have on the Caravette's directional stability.

Whereas VW owners rarely considered the drum brakes anything other than adequate, the writer of this same report experienced 'high deceleration figures in return for easy pedal applications – more effective than the brake tests show them to be'.

When the much larger Bay-Window arrived, Camper conversions became more diverse in their fixtures and fittings.

The majority of interior layouts followed Devon's example, with a central table between two bench seats that converted into a double bed, and wardrobes and cupboard space towards the rear.

Home-from-home convenience – wardrobes were spacious, and the inside of the doors was fitted with a good-sized vanity mirror.

Most Bays had much larger stoves, close to the sliding door; an awning was essential for cooking during inclement weather.

A popular accessory, the front-mounted roofrack was almost essential for foreign family holidays.

With a child's bunk bed and two clothes drawers below it in the area above the engine, the Caravette continued to be one of the best conversions on the British market, and won the hearts of many enthusiasts. To many, both inside and outside the Volkswagen fold, every VW Camper was a Caravette.

The Dormobile

Another name that became synonymous with Volkswagen Campers was Dormobile. This was a real value-for-money product from Martin Walter Ltd, based in Folkestone, Kent. The Dormobile had an ingeniously simple side-elevating roof made of fibreglass, with two skylights cut into it. The collapsible side pieces, or skirt, around the roof were made in hard-wearing plastic, and were capable of repelling the worst excesses of the British climate for many years.

This roof also gave more headroom – 8ft 4½in (255cm) – than any of the other conventional types on the market at that time. However, its installation, as on all types, required the removal of a structural body bracing member; this is one reason why Volkswagen did not involve themselves in the production of Campers. The loss of torsional rigidity in the bodyshell as a result of this surgery was minimal, and the majority of customers were either none the wiser, or were prepared to accept any loss in exchange for the benefits of the elevating roof.

The Martin Walter roof was also useful in that it contained provision for two bunk beds on each side. These were easily erected by lifting a metal tube upwards, which automatically opened another tube to stretch the fabric of the bed into position. Thoughtfully, the Dormobile's manufacturers included a warning light on the dashboard, which flashed if the vehicle was driven without the roof securely closed.

The seats in the central 'living' area faced forwards in two rows for travelling, or otherwise towards the central table. They could be folded flat to make a double bed or two singles. Lighting was provided in the form of fluorescent strips, and conventional electric bulbs above the cooker and in the cab. Although the cooker included a grill, it had no oven; because it was next to the sink, some found it awkward to use, because it was necessary to remove the rear seat to gain access to it.

It is a tight fit, but every available space is cleverly utilized; here, sleeping bags and spare water tanks are stashed beneath the bench seat.

Storage space was provided by cupboards adjacent to the sink, and two further ones high up, close to the roof, for cutlery. The folding dinette table was stored behind the driver when not in use. In July 1962, the

Bays provided ample space above the engine for one or two small children to sleep.

The reality of taking two small children on holiday in a Bus is often at variance with the endearing scene captured by this period Volkswagen publicity shot.

Motor's journalists squeezed a creditable 64mph (102.5km/h) from a Dormobile test vehicle, and overall fuel mileage of 26mpg (10.88l/100km). The consumption was criticized, for being on the 'high' side, as were an axle whine, a squeak from the double side doors, a tendency to wander in sidewinds, and weak headlamps. ('Weak' was hardly the word to describe the Splittie's ability to light the way ahead. More accurately, it was pathetic, woefully inadequate and dreadful.)

Martin Walter side-elevating roofs became available as extra-cost options on a number of other converters' products and, by the mid-1960s, nearly all Campers, including West-falias, were equipped with a 'pop-up' of some kind or another.

The Caravette – Setting the Standard

These were the days before low-cost flights and package holidays to exotic destinations; the Camper provided an opportunity for everyday folk to travel far from home, without the fear of expensive hotel bills. When the 1500cc engine was introduced in 1963, the popularity of all types of Camper spiralled the world over.

By Volkswagen's normal standards, the 1500 Bus felt positively rocket-like. *The Motor*, testing a Devon Caravette in May 1964, described it as 'a comfortable, long-legged and economic family tourer with few equals'. At this time, the Caravette was setting standards in Britain by which all other Campers were judged.

As always, curtains were fitted all round, and interior space utilization was very good, but it was in the attention to detail that the Caravette's designers really excelled. The wardrobe and cupboards had 'burst-proof' catches, to ensure that their doors did not fly open while the vehicle was moving. There was also a 'pop-out' step below the two side

doors, to facilitate entry and exit to the cabin, as well as the amazing luxury of a heated blanket compartment under the rear bench seat. A portable cooker was fitted, which could be used inside or outside, and additional sound-proofing materials helped to keep levels of condensation down.

With a Martin Walter extending roof, and side awning, this vehicle was a superb all-round touring machine. It had the ability to cruise all day, every day, at 70mph (110km/h), so that reaching distant destinations was no longer the grinding slog it had occasionally been with the 1200. With the 1500, Volksfolks really started going places, and no one had cause to moan about 26mpg (10.88l/100km) either.

Camper Adventure

By the middle of this decade of massive social upheaval, the Volkswagen Campers had revolutionized the camping and Camper scene. The influence that Camper Buses had on people cannot be underestimated. In many countries, magazines and newspapers began to publish exciting articles and photographs of great expeditions undertaken by ordinary everyday people in Volkswagens.

In the summer of 1967, the American journal *Popular Imported Cars* published a now-famous article, in which Ernst Jahn wrote of a trip completed by him and his wife and their Bus, from New York to Brazil and back. In response to this article, several more Americans took to the roads on similarly hazardous journeys. The Jahns' seven-month trip took them through twenty-one countries, over nearly 28,000 miles (44,800km), from a lowest point at 235ft (70m) below sea level at Salton Sea in California to 17,384ft (5,215m) above sea level near La Paz, Bolivia. Interestingly, unlike modern Volkswagens (including Mexican-

Five types of elevating roof (this page and opposite): *the front-hinged Westfalia.*

built Beetles), the Bus's carburettor settings did not need to be adjusted in order to cope with the thin air at altitude.

Jahn wrote that 'the car climbed the steep grades of the world's highest highway from Lima to La Oroya with astonishing ease'.

Many of the roads en route were constructed of nothing more than cobbled stones and boulders, yet the Bus coped almost without incident. Jahn added,

> People everywhere were quite surprised to see a foreign car equipped with a bed, kitchen and refrigerator, not to mention the running water. Many times we were surrounded during lunch stops or in the evenings and had to demonstrate our mobile home.

Specialist publications in Britain and the Commonwealth began to publish similar articles, and it was not long before Australians and New Zealanders started making journeys from home to Britain in VW Buses. Invariably, the journey would terminate alongside the pavement outside their respective embassy in London. Here, the weary

Side elevator by Martin Walter Ltd.

Rectangular box type by Devon.

Rear-hinged Westfalia.

The fixed fibreglass roof that became popular in the 1980s.

Caravan-type bodies were built by GT in Britain, Jurgens of South Africa and Karmann in Germany.

travellers – dozens at a time by the mid-1970s – would put a 'For Sale' notice on the Camper, and wait for a potential purchaser to fund a one-way ticket for the long plane ride home.

The Multicar

As the VW Camper way of life became more popular, home-produced conversions continued at an astonishing rate. In Britain, specialist company, Danbury Conversions of Chelmsford, Essex, came up with the Multicar. This vehicle offered seating for up to eight, and sleeping accommodation for four children and three adults with the use of the collapsible side tent.

As the interior fittings and fixtures were all easily removed, a number of seating and sleeping permutations was possible with this conversion. *The Motor* tested a Multicar over 1,500 miles (2,400km) in May 1967, just

before the end of Splittie production, and summed up life in a Camper rather well. The writer commented as follows:

> We started off feeling rather cramped in the Multicar but, as we got the hang of the movable units, it turned out to be quite spacious, even under bad weather conditions. In fine weather, with the canopy over the double doors at one side, it was a very pleasant way to live. The two-burner-and-grill cooker was satisfactory in operation, but in bad weather when the doors were shut up, the atmosphere became somewhat oppressive and condensation heavy on metal fittings.

THE ALTERNATIVE SOCIETY

In the first thirty years of Volkswagen Campers, journalists who tested them generally agreed on their good points, and on some of their disadvantages. A recurring theme in many reports was the idea that a Camper could, in theory at least, provide a home on a full-time basis for anyone prepared to put up with a few discomforts.

Most owners were content to use their Buses for the odd camping weekends away and longer holidays. To a few, however, a Bus is home. Reformed heroin addict Ian Flynn, from Liverpool, has lived in his home-converted 1967 Kombi for more than ten years. Having achieved national fame for his leadership in protests over new road-building schemes, Flynn (as he likes to be known) rejects a conventional way of life out of hand. His VW is an integral part of his 'New Age' travelling lifestyle. The son of a Merseyside policeman, he, like so many living in inner-city areas without the prospect of finding employment, quickly drifted into drug addiction. Having witnessed the death of so many friends from drug abuse, he eventually kicked his habit, and went out on the road in the Bus.

The long-wheelbase Dutch-built Kemperink is rare, but makes for an ideal Camper home.

'There was a time not long ago when I had nothing to my name except the Camper,' he says. 'It provided me with a home when there was nowhere else to go – it was like a friend that never let me down – and although it looks pretty ratty in its "battleship grey" paint, it goes as well as ever.'

Flynn still lives in his Bus with his partner, Liz, a business management graduate, and their small child. With funding from a government grant, they work in the timber industry, the Camper doubling as a tow vehicle and general workhorse, as well as a roof over their heads at night.

CAMPING BAYS

By the time Split-Screen production finished, the VW Camper was established the world over as the market leader, although it was generally smaller and slower than its rivals, had less interior space, and had an air-cooled engine that some considered to be too noisy. When the Bay was launched in 1967, its larger size gave Westfalia and the independent converters, who had performed marvels within the confines of the Splittie, even more design opportunities.

With the introduction of the Bay, the purchase price of the Camper rose accordingly. In North America, the Westfalia was priced at $2,700–3,000, and in Britain a typical Dormobile from Martin Walter was around £1,300, depending on specification. Despite the dip in West Germany's economic fortunes in the mid-1960s, the Westfalias sold well, both on the home market and in North America. Even though these vehicles were more expensive, few genuine Camper enthusiasts complained. The cost of an average saloon or estate car, without beds, cooker and refrigerator, was roughly the same. For devotees and increasing numbers of converts, the new Bay Campers were little short of a miracle.

145

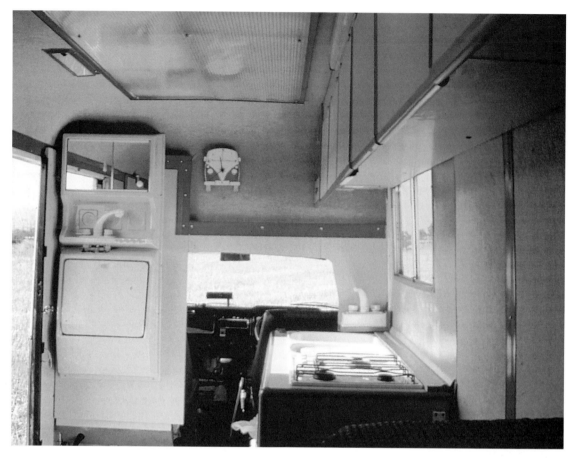

The Kemperink's interior, designed to sleep four, is luxurious, amazingly spacious and wholly self-contained.

The Sportsmobile

Manufacturers continued to compete to find the most efficient way of utilizing available space, and there were one or two new companies on the scene, including Andrews Inc, of Indiana, USA.

Andrews produced a Microbus-based Sportsmobile. It was an outstanding vehicle, which could be supplied ready converted, or with the interior fittings as a kit for home assembly. Andrews also converted Panelvans, removing sheet metal from the body for the purpose of fitting window glass.

The Sportsmobile was available with a large oblong elevating roof, dubbed 'the Penthouse', which gave a useful 7ft (2.1m) of headroom. Accessories at extra cost included a large tent and a refrigerator. Designed to sleep two adults and up to four children – two in the cab and two in the Penthouse – this model was one of few independently built US conversions, and a budget alternative to the Westfalia. The Sportsmobile was also one of the first Campers to have its spare wheel attached to the front nose panel, thereby allowing for a little more space in the rear luggage compartment above the engine.

Kemperink

For those who required much more space than a standard Bus could offer, there was a small selection of larger commercials from other manufacturers. The Dutch Kemperink outfit catered specially for those who wanted lorry-type space, but who did not want to leave the Volkswagen fold.

Kemperinks were bespoke conversions with a longer wheelbase – up to 4ft (1.2m) in some cases – and a vast box-shaped body. To support the extra weight of the body, and improve its torsional rigidity, the chassis was reinforced with strong box-section channels. Kemperink had produced a small number of Splittie conversions, but the Bay-Window versions, although rare, were much more popular.

Generally, the company was more involved in building vehicles for tradespeople – including bakers, butchers, grocers – but the majority of survivors have been converted to Campers in private hands. Because of this, the specification of each differs from that of the next. The best-known of the few that can still be seen regularly at VW Shows in Europe and Britain is the red and white example belonging to Simon Holloway (a leading light in the British Type 2 Club), from Oxfordshire.

With a larger sliding side door, and a massive, top-hinged tailgate, access to the interior is exceptional. Interior equipment is almost on a par with what anyone might have at home. It has four berths – more could be accommodated with ease – a fridge, cooker, hot and cold running water, toilet facilities, and almost unlimited cupboard space, and few Campers come close to the versatility of this Kemperink.

The GT

Another rarity among the 'big boys' was the GT Motorized model, produced in Hull.

The GT outfit produced special Camper bodies for a number of vehicles, including Talbots, Bedfords and the Leyland Sherpa, and for a small number of Bay-Window Volkswagens. Unusually, the Panelvan was chosen as the basis for the conversion, with most of its bodywork (with the obvious exception of the cab) being cut away. In its place was a large body made of aluminium-alloy, styled along the lines of a conventional trailer caravan.

The Panelvan's standard sills (rocker panels) were also removed, and replaced by strong box-section pieces to support the body, which, despite its lightweight construction, was quite heavy. Unlike the Kemperink, the GT had a hinged side door, for access to the rear cabin. At the back of the body there was a top-hinged, double-glazed window extending across the width of the vehicle to allow entry to the rear luggage space.

Engine-cooling was taken care of by a plastic scoop on each side of the body behind the rear wheels, which ducted cool air through apertures in the body to the engine's cooling fan. The interior was not as spacious as the Kemperink, but the GT Motorized could sleep up to five in splendid comfort. A double bunk was housed in the overhanging part of the body above the cab, there was a double bed in the rear over the engine, and a single bed across the width of the vehicle, behind the cab seats.

Two dining tables were provided, as were a full-height wardrobe close to the side door, and cupboards at head height all the way around the body. Like so many Campers in the 1970s, the GT had a fully pressurized water system, a refrigerator, two-burner gas stove and grill, and a toilet. However, this vehicle also had a gas fire, a television socket and an aerial attachment. In short, this was a serious attempt to combine a caravan body and a motorized chassis.

Very few GTs were built and the only known survivor is a 2-litre, owned by Phil Shaw, secretary of the British Type 2 Club. It is a 1975 conversion on a 1972 Panelvan, showing that GT, like many other independents, did not rely solely on brand-new vehicles for conversion work. Despite the bulk and shape of what at first appears to be a rather ungainly body, Phil's vehicle will cruise easily above 80mph (125km/h).

A body similar to that of the GT was available in South Africa, from the Jurgens company.

Max Headroom

A great advantage of the Kemperink, GT and Jurgens was that the height of their bodies gave enough headroom for the tallest people, without the need for an extending or elevating roof. Standard vehicles with or without a 'pop-up' were, with the arguable exception of the excellent Martin Walter side elevator, always compromised. In Splittie days, Westfalia provided a square, turret-like elevating roof. It gave sufficient headroom, but was small; standing in it felt rather like wearing an oversize 'pork pie' hat.

For the Bay-Windows, Westfalia came up with a more satisfactory solution, in the form of a tilting fibreglass roof. This was hinged at the front just above the top of the windscreen, and opened upwards at the rear to give reasonable headroom throughout its length. From the mid-1970s, this arrangement was reversed, so that it was hinged at the rear, and opened upwards from the front.

Third-generation Wedge Campers were more civilized, more sophisticated and considerably more expensive.

Westfalia's Bay

As ever, the Westfalia came with good-quality equipment, including a fridge, kitchen sink, and icebox cabinet housed on top of the water container. A food storage cupboard next to the icebox had a cover, which, when lifted out, doubled as a work surface. A gas stove was an extra-cost option of which most customers availed themselves. There was also the option of a large, rectangular free-standing tent, big enough to sleep three adults, to be attached to the side of the body.

With its wood-panelled interior, two tables, reading lamp, louvred rear side windows, wardrobes and all-round curtains, Westfalia's Campmobile remained among the very best conversions. As on most Campers, removing all the special equipment was easy and quick, if it was necessary to revert the vehicle to a people or cargo carrier.

CAPE CAMPERS

The Kombi Kamper

Volkswagen South Africa, which ran its own affairs with little interference from the parent company in Germany, produced its own range of vehicles in a purpose-built factory. Unlike the equivalent Beetles, South African-built Buses differed little from their German counterparts.

Dubbed the Kombi Kamper, but actually based on the Microbus, it boasted light woodgrain-covered furniture, comprising a full-length wardrobe fitted with a vanity mirror, a fold-away dining table, storage cupboards, and drawers for cutlery and crockery. A large formica worktop was erected over storage cupboards behind the driver. The rear bench seat folded outwards towards the centre of the vehicle to form a double bed, and a hammock was provided in

Wedge interiors were more comfortable; many had velour upholstery.

the cab to sleep one child; the other child's sleeping place was in the rear luggage space above the engine.

All the wooden interior panels were insulated, to protect against condensation, but a cooker and fridge were extra-cost options. An elevating roof was not available at any cost. During the 1970s, these vehicles became highly sought after all over the African continent, along with Beetles, Land Rovers and the rugged, reliable Peugeot 504 saloon. VW Campers were particularly favoured by doctors and vets practising in remote areas, whose rounds could take them hundreds of miles from home. With

the Camper, it was possible to carry large supplies of medicines, and there was always a bed for the night in the back.

However, the lack of an elevating roof really annoyed some customers. T.Y. Thomson, an assistant port captain from Cape Town, spent several years scouring the globe for a sleeper cabin, capable of housing four children, for the top of his Bus. No manufacturer – even in Britain – could fulfil his demand, so he constructed his own.

A large structure made from aluminium-alloy, which nearly doubled the height of the vehicle, the assembly was designed to fold down flat by pulling on a series of hoists. Access to the 'turret' was through the standard factory-fitted sunroof. Thomson's turret did indeed sleep four children, in addition to two adults down below, in the normal way, and appeared to offer a good solution to his problem. He attempted to market his complex design, but it was expensive, and the majority of South Africans plumped instead for the inconvenience of the standard Camper.

The Auto-villa

Another South African company, Jurgens Caravans, based in Kempton Park, Transvaal, produced a version of the Bay Camper similar to the British GT model. Based on the Kombi, the Jurgens Auto-Villa had an alloy trailer caravan-type body, and the first example appeared in 1973.

The Jurgens model was built under licence in both Germany and Brazil, by Karmann. The Osnabrück-based coach-builder had many years' experience in bespoke coachwork, and had enjoyed great success with the Beetle Cabriolet and Karmann

The choice in Wedge Campers was bewildering, despite the headline on this period advertisement.

Ghia, but the motorized caravan was a new departure. It came about as a result of a visit by Wilhelm Karmann to South Africa. He spotted an example of the Jurgens Auto-Villa, contacted the company that built it, and sought permission for a licence.

A superb vehicle, the Auto-Villa had the Bay's original engine-cooling louvres cleverly built into the body, behind the rear side windows. A four-berth vehicle with a double bed over the driver's cab (access to which was up a removable ladder), the interior boasted almost unrivalled facilities.

South African publication *Car* tested a 2-litre version in 1979 and remarked, 'One of its endearing features is a walk-through ability from the cab to the caravan area – entering into another world as you do so. The design is magnificent, making the fullest use of every centimetre of space to create a comfortable and self-contained living area, complete with kitchenette and cloakroom compartment.'

Toilet facilities housed in a separate 'cloakroom' included a cabinet, mirror, optional chemical loo, and even a footbath. The fully equipped kitchen was situated between the side door and the cab, and had a large cooker, and a fridge, and storage cupboards containing sufficient crockery for six. Two gas bottles served the cooker, and water was drawn to the sink and washbasin by an electric pump. Lighting was by no fewer than three fluorescent tubes. So much electrical equipment made for easy and convenient camping but, as several owners discovered, could quickly drain even a 12-volt battery.

The dining area was sited at the back of the body, with a removable table and seating for up to six. The seats converted easily into a double bed or two singles. The whole body was insulated with foam, and the interior was finished in expensive hardwood veneer. One feature not usually found on Campers,

151

but doubtless appreciated by South Africans, was insect-proof netting attached to the sliding window in the side door.

Despite its weight and large frontal area, *Car* magazine recorded acceptable performance figures for this Bus. Top speed worked out at around 75mph (120km/h), and 50mph (80km/h) was achieved from rest in 19.1 seconds.

BACK IN BLIGHTY

During the 1970s, British converters led the VW Camper field, and the Devons were generally at the top of the tree. By 1979, Devon's range-topping Moonraker was a genuine 80mph (128km/h) vehicle with hitherto unknown levels of equipment. However, the 2-litre version with side-elevating roof, brake servo and fridge worked out at a cool £7,300. To put this figure into perspective, a perfectly serviceable used Daytona Ferrari – the classic of the road-going front-engined Ferraris – could be had at the time for £2,000 less!

With the elevating fibreglass roof supported on gas-filled struts and running the entire length of the vehicle, there was more bedroom and headroom space than ever. Two children's bunks were contained within the roof, which ran across the width of the Bus, yet there was still plenty of headroom over the kitchen and dining area. The adult double bed was made up in the usual manner, by folding the rear seat outwards.

Innovations included a dining table supported by a single central leg, which fitted into a socket embedded in the floor, and a cooker with a folding flap that doubled as a small work surface. To create additional space in the rear, the spare wheel was mounted externally at the rear above the bumper, and needed to be removed in order to access the engine.

Storage space was provided by a wardrobe behind the front passenger, and a number of cupboards and shelves were attached to the right-hand side of the interior. Apart from the rear bench seat, there were two further seats – a fold-out in the wardrobe, and another one attached to the outside of the wardrobe. In place of the standard Volkswagen's vinyl seat covers in the cab, the Moonraker had more comfortable nylon upholstery, and carpeting throughout to match. These were luxury touches clearly designed to help the brand stay a step or two ahead.

When Peter Noad tested the Moonraker for VW *Safer Motoring* magazine in 1979, he found that its performance was roughly the same as that of the Volkswagen Polo 1100cc model. Where the Bus lost out, though, was on fuel consumption, which had dipped to 22mpg (12.8l/100km).

THE CULT CONTINUES

By the time the Bay bowed out, in 1979, motor caravans had become big business for a number of companies. Annual trade shows sprang up on both sides of the Atlantic, one of the biggest taking place in Britain at large venues such as Brands Hatch. Camper Buses became increasingly expensive and better-equipped. One-off custom jobs were becoming popular, and there was seemingly no ceiling on an acceptable purchase price.

In some quarters, the Bus's purpose had also changed. Many VW devotees still used their Buses for camping purposes, but clubs also started to organize exclusive Bus weekend gatherings. These meetings continue to this day, and it is quite common for several hundreds of vehicles to congregate in one place, their owners swapping stories on related Volkswagen topics.

By the time of the launch of the third-generation Wedges, in 1979, the VW Camper cult had been set in concrete foundations. In 1987, the importance of the VW Camper was recognized by the Henry Ford Museum of Transport in Dearborn, Michigan. The museum considered that the Camper had been solely responsible for creating the post-war recreational vehicle lifestyle in the USA. A Split-Screen Westfalia was presented to the museum by Volkswagen of America, and is said to have 'filled a vital gap in the museum's history of road transport'.

FULL STEAM AHEAD

Both the Splittie and the Bay had served their purpose, but when the Wedge – now also considered a classic – came along, camping weekends became very much a home-from-home affair. The additional size

of the body made the interior exceptionally spacious, and there was an expanded choice in accessories and fittings. The larger tailgate and side sliding door gave easy access to the rear and cabin respectively.

Westfalia in Germany remained the official converter, and the majority of Americans were content to stick with the company they had come to know and love. By this time, there were three official converters in Britain – Autohomes, Autosleepers and Richard Holdsworth – and all produced vehicles for the luxury end of the market. The Devons continued, but were beginning to look decidedly basic in their appointments, in comparison with some conversions.

Up until 1980, elevating roofs were as popular as ever – Danbury were the first to make a power-operated one – but, thereafter, high-top fibreglass roofs became much more common. Westfalia's Vanagon

When the water-cooled Wedges arrived in 1982, the search for the perfect elevating roof continued unabated.

model, which, incidentally, had cab seats that could be swivelled round to face the rear, soldiered on with a roof hinged at the rear that tilted upwards from the front. But many manufacturers favoured a roof that gave sufficient headroom throughout the length of the vehicle on a permanent basis.

Fabric-skirted elevators went out of fashion, despite the problems of garaging a vehicle with a permanently lofty high-top. Converters had differing opinions as to the correct design for the new-style roofs. Autosleepers and Holdsworth roofs added around 6in (15cm) to the overall height of the Bus, while the Autohomes Kamper was a whole foot (30cm) taller.

Roofs varied in shape too, and, although some of the boxier types had a pronounced effect on handling in a sidewind, none was badly designed. Before 1980, high-roofs with the correct aerodynamic profile at the front end included RGA and Bariban. After 1980, the choice became much greater. Holdsworth used Volkswagen's own make, a boxy but spacious affair, whereas Autohomes and Autosleepers used roofs with swept-back front and stepped rear sections, which had a built-in roof rack for carrying extra luggage. RGA made a roof that resembled an upturned boat, while Diamond RV produced a sleekly profiled unit. The Sheldon roof was favoured by the smaller companies; like Volkswagen's, this roof was high from front to rear, but without swage lines.

In addition to these popular roofs, there were many small companies – often one-man bands – producing dozens of variations on the same theme. All worked in fibreglass, because modifications were much easier to make, as and when they were required.

The choice was enormous and, such is the popularity of the air-cooled Wedge, there are today a number of firms engaged in restoring these vehicles (particularly Panelvans), and fitting them with high-tops and camping equipment.

By 1982, when the last of the classic air-cooled Buses was produced, all Camper conversions were to a very high specification. All, virtually without exception, came with a cooker, a fridge, sleeping accommodation for four or more, a fully equipped kitchen, expensive floor coverings, velour upholstery, a fire extinguisher, a toilet and a pressurized water system. The only major difference between each Bus was the location of all that equipment.

7 On the Fringe

UTILITY VEHICLES

Right from its inception, it was obvious that the Transporter's usefulness and versatility extended well beyond its main intended role of ferrying people and cargo. As Germany was gradually rebuilt after the Second World War, the service industries found increasingly diverse reasons to buy specially converted VW Buses.

The first examples included Volkswagen-built ambulances and fire tenders. By the mid-1950s, virtually all the specialist trades had begun to order vehicles equipped especially

Volkswagen made a specially equipped ambulance version from 1951. Very few saw active service outside the Germanic countries.

for their purposes, and there was no shortage of independent companies willing to cater for their every need. Relatively few of these special vehicles were exported outside Europe. The ambulance version was eventually made available on the British and other markets, but public utilities are notoriously patriotic when it comes to buying fleet transport, and there were few takers outside Germany, Austria and Switzerland. Because of their rarity, those export examples that survived are much coveted by collectors today. Those that were sold on the home market are also much sought after; being strictly for utility purposes, they led such a hard life that the majority of them were driven into the ground.

The Ambulance

Based on the Kombi, the first Volkswagen-built ambulances appeared just after Christmas 1951. Always painted in white, these vehicles differed from the regular Kombi in that the rear door was hinged at the bottom, opening out from the top. This formed a convenient platform on which a patient on a stretcher could be laid and more easily manoeuvred into the cabin.

Despite its popularity with the German health authorities, the VW, with its rear engine, did not make for an ideal ambulance. More conventional vehicles in Britain, and elsewhere, were larger, had double rear

The blue flashing light and roof-mounted air horns were extra-cost options.

doors and a walk-in ramp for convenience. On the other hand, the Kombi's comparative lightness gave it superior performance.

The special equipment on board varied from hospital to hospital, and was dependent largely on the purpose for which the vehicle was used. Generally, there was a couple of stretchers, two chairs for medical staff, medicine storage cabinets and a step below the sill to aid entry through the side doors. In the absence of a high-top or elevating roof, it must have been rather cramped for the doctors and nurses whose job it was to work within the confines of the Splittie ambulance. However, the ride comfort offered by torsion-bar springing was of benefit to patients, and a great improvement on the cart-sprung boneshakers of the pre-war era.

From a space point of view, the Bay-Window version was a great improvement, although restricted headroom continued to cause inconvenience. Bays also differed from Splitties in that their tailgates were standard top-hinged Kombi items, access for staff and patients being much easier through the sliding side door. Features included the normal medicine cabinets, a partition wall between the cab and 'cargo' compartment, with a sliding window built into it, bench seats behind the cab facing the rear, a brace of stretchers, chairs and fluorescent lighting.

In addition, there were formica-topped work surfaces, floor-covering material that was easy to disinfect, a step that operated automatically when the sliding door was opened, and several hooks around the interior walls, from which blood plasma could be suspended.

By the time the 2-litre engine arrived, in the mid-1970s, the ambulance was a genuine 80mph (128km/h) cross-country vehicle. Although it was not the equal in performance of the 110mph (175km/h) Citroën CX estate cars favoured by French medical authorities, it was considerably quicker than the ungainly Bedfords used in Britain. Wedge versions were similarly well equipped, and bigger, with better access.

Military Vehicles

A military version was, understandably, a late addition to the range of special Buses. After the war, the victorious Allies did not want to allow Germany – a nation that had twice tried to conquer the world – the luxury of an army that might have a third crack at it.

Bay-Window military vehicles were, however, supplied to the German armed forces, in the guise of Kombis, Panelvans and Pick-Ups. Again, these vehicles differed in specification depending on their intended purpose. First-aid kits, black-out covers for the lights and window glass, and rifle attachments were normal features. The suspension was made stronger, to cope with carrying heavy weights over rough ground, and the bodies were painted in the army's normal colour of olive green and khaki. In training exercises, these vehicles proved time and time again that they were worth more than the sum of their parts. They were able to withstand prolonged periods of abuse without breaking. However, they would have benefited enormously from four-wheel drive.

Fire Tenders

Resplendent in their pillar-box red livery, fire tenders were an early addition to the range. Outside Germany, Split-Screen versions are extremely rare. In common with the military vehicles and ambulances, the fire tenders had beefed-up suspension, to cope with the formidable weight of the special equipment on board, which also took

The pillar-box red fire tender was not able to carry as much equipment as a traditional appliance, but it was much quicker to the scene.

up a great deal of space in the cargo compartment. This included a generator, cutting equipment, water pump and hoses, protective clothing and a ladder, and left space for just three fire-fighting personnel in the cab.

Despite their drawbacks, these vehicles were exceptionally useful because, like the ambulance, they were quicker than the larger, heavier, conventional appliances.

One appliance of which the German fire service might have availed itself, but did not, was a Bus Pick-Up with an extending gantry on the rear bed. Such vehicles did exist, but they had been purpose-built for the repair of overhead cables and street lighting.

Bay-Window fire tenders were purpose-built, rather than adapted, and could carry much more equipment.

Fire-fighting equipment at the rear made extensive bodywork modifications necessary.

THE 'KLEINLIEFERWAGEN' (THE MINI VAN)

Of all the special-bodied Buses, the officially designated Type 147 model was the most diverse. It was designed by Volkswagen, and built by Westfalia at the latter's Wiedenbruck plant, specially for the Deutsche Bundespost (the German Federal Post Office). The Post Office had been one of Volkswagen's best customers but, as the years went by, it became clear to the postal authorities that a purpose-built vehicle was required for delivering mail.

The 147 Kleinlieferwagen – popularly known as the 'Fridolin' – was a full series production model produced in relatively low numbers between 1964 and 1973. The German Post Office bought 6,139 units (85 per cent of the total production), while 1,201 went to the Swiss Post Office. A small number of the Swiss ones were used in Liechtenstein.

The Fridolin was unmistakably a Volkswagen and air-cooled but, as it was required for delivering small items of mail, it was nowhere near as big as the regular Transporter, and had a more box-like body. In relation to the size of the body, the sliding cab door on each side was enormous and gave much easier access to the cargo area.

This little van was 5in (8cm) wider and 9in (14.5cm) taller than a Beetle, and 3in (5cm) narrower and 8in (13cm) shorter than the standard Transporter. It made for a remarkably compact vehicle. Kombis and Panelvans had roughly double the load capacity but, as far as the German Post Office was concerned, the 147 was ideally suited to its purpose.

From the front, the styling resembled the Type 3 saloon, but it was more like the normal Transporter from the rear. Because it was only required to travel at low speed, the Beetle's 34bhp 1200 engine and gearbox were fitted at the rear, while the fuel tank, windscreen-washer bottle and spare wheel sat under the bonnet at the front – also in Beetle fashion.

The windscreen was a large curved one-piece panoramic item from the Type 3. The wheels, hubcaps, suspension, instruments, controls and seat – only the driver got a seat unless one for a passenger was specified – were all from the Bus and Beetle parts bins at Hanover and Wolfsburg. Based on the floorpan of the Type 34 Karmann Ghia ('Razor-Edge' model), which was wider than those used in the other VW Models, the 147 had excellent interior storage facilities.

In effect, the 147 was even more of a box on wheels than the original box on wheels. It was inherently slab-sided, and the monotony

The 'Kleinlieferwagen', or Type 147 mini van, was built for postal duties in Germany. This example is one of the few to come to Britain, and awaits restoration.

of the sheet metalwork was only broken by a prominent swage line, running from the top of the front wheel arch to the rear. The horizontally cut engine-cooling louvres sat on the sides of the vehicle towards the rear, just below the 'waistband', and a standard Transporter engine lid was hinged at the rear.

Curiously, the sides of the bodywork behind the cab included a pressing for windows, but it is unlikely that Westfalia ever made a production model with side windows. The Swiss version had wrap-around rear windows in Splittie Samba style, but there were very few examples like this.

Functional and austere, the 147 offered the driver little in the way of creature comforts. The cab floor was covered with a rubber mat,

the interior door panels were in fabric-covered hardboard, the other interior panels were painted in body colour, and there were heater vents in the front sills only. No heating was ducted to the rear, and a sun visor was fitted to the driver's side only.

Apart from wrap-around rear side windows, the Swiss version also had a much larger rear window in the tailgate and, for security purposes, vertical metal bars fitted behind the glass. In deference to the Swiss winter weather, an Eberspächer petrol heater was available as an extra-cost option. Whereas the majority of vehicles supplied to the German Post Office were painted in yellow, Swiss examples had a yellow lower body, silver upper, and a black painted central waistband. Swiss vehicles were also commonly fitted with a roofrack, and a single reversing lamp above the left-hand light cluster.

As the post offices in Germany and Switzerland bought new Fridolins year on year, used ones were sold off into the hands of private traders. With their shelving and storage cupboards, they were useful as delivery vehicles and mobile shops of all types but, like so many commercial vehicles, they led a hard life and are consequently now rare. A handful and no more made their way into non-Germanic countries; one or two have ended up in Britain. Well-respected Volkswagen writer and historian Jerry Sloniger tested one of these vehicles for *Foreign Car Guide* in 1965, and was particularly struck by its engineering quality, marvelling at how its sliding door 'clunked' into place so precisely. He also commented,

> Even a quick look at the van layout and compactness, while thinking of such metropolitan needs (and traffic jams) and you wonder only that nobody got such a good idea before. By reducing the overall bulk they achieve roughly the same performance in the van with a 1.2-litre engine as the larger Kombi with 1.5 litres. Both are rated at 60mph [95km/h], depending on the way the wind is blowing.

The most important point about Sloniger's test was not necessarily what he wrote, but that he bothered to write it at all. After all, he had no need to. The vehicle was built for the Post Office, the Post Office was happy with it, it was not on general release to the public, and there was absolutely no reason why anyone should know what a Fridolin was. The fact that *Foreign Car Guide* published Sloniger's report, and presumably paid him for it, is indicative of the high esteem in which Volkswagen's products were held.

The 147 van could not be described as pretty but, in as much as it was designed and developed for a specific use, it was a perfect piece for the period in which it saw service. Interestingly, similarly styled right-hand drive vehicles are used to this day in certain states of the USA for delivering mail.

THE 'ODDBALLS'

Almost every trade and industry, particularly in Germany, Austria and Switzerland, found a use for the Transporter. A number of specialist companies sprang up in the 1950s, manufacturing special bodies and equipment to cater for every conceivable need. No model in the range was safe from the attentions of the special builders, but the Pick-Up and the Panelvan proved to be the most popular bases for the majority of conversions.

They included Pick-Ups with a hydraulically-operated tipping bed – popular with builders and gardeners – box bodies with a side serving hatch for the mobile catering trade, a similar, refrigerated body for butchers and fishmongers, and a rather bizarre mobile milking machine for farmers who, in the days before intensive farming methods, found it easier to milk cows in the fields rather than driving them into a shed.

The German police authorities used Kombis fitted with radar equipment to track speeding motorists, and both Panelvans and Kombis were used for general police work on and off the motorway network. These vehicles were also used for the same purpose in Switzerland and Austria.

Of all the special-purpose Transporters, the extended load carrier was one of the relatively few built by Volkswagen. These were based on both the single- and double-cab Pick-Ups, and came with a box-trailer attached to the back of the vehicle with a long towbar. These were used extensively in Europe by the forestry authorities, timber and building trades, as they were ideal for hauling long tree trunks, scaffolding and pipework.

A support cradle for the front end of the load was attached to the bed. The design of the cradle was modified down the years, but it basically comprised a steel frame with hawser tightening ratchets for securing the load. The metal-framed wood-panelled box-trailer also had a cradle fitted with tightening ratchets.

As an alternative to the box-trailer, there was a wheeled cradle frame, and this was also attached to the vehicle by a long tow-bar. Usefully, the towbar was adjustable for length. The great thing about the extended load carriers was that they were able to carry enormous quantities of cargo, equipment and, in the case of the double-cab Pick-Up, up to six people as well.

The specials were by no means confined to Germany, Austria and Switzerland. Pick-Ups with a manually, or electrically operated loading platform were popular with members of the motor trade in British Commonwealth countries. In Australia and New Zealand, Pick-Ups were also turned into small stock lorries, simply by attaching a steel cage to the cargo bed. In most countries, glaziers found the task of transporting large pieces of glass easy, after attaching large, near-vertical frames to the sides of their Pick-Ups.

Mobile workshops, dental surgeries, post offices and libraries – the VW Bus was used for all of these purposes in all four corners of the globe.

THE CUSTOM BUSES

Away from the mainstream of standard vehicles is a large and ever-growing army of VW enthusiasts devoted to the art of customizing, a trend that started in the USA during the 1950s. People like Joe Vittone, of the EMPI tuning company, and Gene Berg began manufacturing tuning parts for air-cooled Volkswagens, many for the benefit of those who raced Beetles on quarter-mile drag strips. (Racing driver Dan Gurney, the only man ever to win a Grand Prix for Porsche, was another one of these people.)

Of all the many customizing fashions and phases that have come and gone over the past thirty-five years or so, the most enduring is the 'Cal-look', from California. Although this distinctive style of modification began with the Beetle, it is every bit as popular today with Bus owners. Lowered suspension, a powerful engine, alloy road wheels, de-chromed bodywork traditionally finished in pastel or bright primary colours, and tailor-made upholstery are all hallmarks of the California style.

There have been dozens of variations on the same theme, and the original idea has been developed to suit individual tastes. None of the models is considered to be too utilitarian for this customizing treatment, and even a single-cab Pick-Up can be transformed into a road-burning object of automotive art.

The Cal-look is not just about modifying Buses and Beetles. In the same way that the Camper became part of a distinctive lifestyle for its followers, so too has Cal-look. It is a lifestyle in which sea, sand and surf play equally important parts. During the 1970s, hundreds of clubs devoted to Cal-look vehicles sprang up on both sides of the Atlantic. They regularly organize meetings, rallies and cruises, and a lucrative industry has grown up around their activities.

Cal-look originally grew from California-based company EMPI (European Motor Products Inc), founded by Joe Vittone. Apart from selling Okrasa and Denzel tuning products for Volkswagens, Vittone manufactured his own anti-roll bars. After meeting English racing driver Graham Hill, whose company Speedwell also manufactured tuning components, Vittone came to a mutually convenient business deal between the two firms. They swapped and marketed each other's 'goodies'. Shorrocks superchargers, 5in-wide BRM magnesium-alloy wheels, twin carburettors and a host of other parts were quickly added to both Speedwell and EMPI's lists of tuning accessories. As a result, Bus and Beetle owners discovered that their vehicles could be made to travel more quickly than the people at the Volkswagen factories had ever dreamed.

Vittone and business associate Dean Lowry worked closely and successfully together for many years, developing all

manner of tuning kits and accessories for VWs. They also went drag racing in Beetles, and were partially responsible for one of the many cults that has grown up around these unique vehicles. The original EMPI company was closed down in 1974, but the name was eventually sold, and parts bearing the famous appellation are still available.

The late Gene Berg was the other famous VW tuning man. His company, based in Orange County, began manufacturing high-quality parts and tuning VWs during the 1960s. Special crankshafts, twin carburettors, close-ratio gearboxes and tuned exhausts produced by the Berg empire have proved to be among the most popular items with the drag-racing and

Of all the customizing styles, Cal-look is the most enduring. Fitted with Fuchs 5-spoke alloys and denuded of bright trim, this Samba Bus is a shining example of the theme.

A remarkably original French-registered Samba complete with bright trim, but the lowered suspension and Fuchs wheels still qualify it for Cal-look.

Cal-look fraternities, because of their impeccable quality and resilience.

The look and feel created by hot-rodders and drag racers had been around for many years, but it was only when freelance photographer Jere Alhadeff wrote an article for *Hot VWs* magazine, in February 1975, that the name 'Cal-look' was officially recognized. At this time, many customized Volkswagens were characterized by wide wheels, lots of body chrome and multi-coloured paint schemes; after Alhadeff's piece about the subtleties of Cal-look, the brash, wide-wheeled monsters went out of fashion almost overnight.

As the Cal-look style caught on – it spread like wildfire from the mid-1980s – the aim was to customize Buses, Karmann Ghias and the Type 3 and 4 saloons in such a way that the beauty of the original product was enhanced. Removing the bumpers and de-chroming the bodywork showed off the original styling lines, making the most of what many regarded as the world's best-looking vehicles.

The interiors on the early vehicles were retained in fairly standard trim, apart from the addition of a tachometer and oil-temperature gauge if a powerful engine was fitted, and a sports steering wheel. As EMPI and Speedwell progressed, more and more vehicles were fitted with a full range of instruments (except, of course, a water-temperature gauge), sports seats, different gear shifters and, more recently, CD players with hugely powerful speakers.

Although the expensive five-bolt BRM alloy wheels were part of the classic look for aficionados, they became less popular after Volkswagen introduced four-bolt wheels on the Beetle, in August 1967. As a result of this, EMPI manufactured an attractive alternative in the form of eight-spoke alloy wheels, in addition to their own five-spoke five-bolt wheels.

Today, EMPI-style wheels are the most popular among Bus and Beetle owners, although many owners favour the equally attractive Fuchs five-spoke alloys traditionally fitted to the Porsche 911. To reinforce the drag-racing connection – illusory in some cases – whatever wheels are chosen are shod with considerably wider tyres at the rear than at the front.

Many Cal-look enthusiasts aim for aesthetically sound modifications, keeping a standard engine, but others lust after power. Today, there are engine-tuning kits and 'bolt-on' barrels and pistons ranging from 1.7 right through to 3 litres. In their most powerful format, with a turbocharger and nitrous-oxide injection, some tuning specialists have extracted more than 600bhp from the venerable flat-four. These engines are mind-blowingly expensive, notoriously short-lived, and wholly inappropriate for street use, but they allow serious drag racers to record almost unbelievable times.

The VW Bus may not seem the ideal shape and weight for a drag-racing machine, but this does not prevent Volksfolks from

The classic 5-spoke EMPI alloy wheels fitted to this Kombi are much imitated by independent manufacturers today.

turning the humble Transporter into a fire-breathing, street-legal Cal-looker. In recent times, there has been a move away from denuding the bodyshell of its standard bright trim, but lowered suspension, alloy wheels, custom upholstery and re-worked power units are here to stay.

POSTSCRIPT: TOWARDS A NEW FUTURE

When the water-cooled engines that powered Transporters from 1982 onwards were announced, VW enthusiasts suffered badly from the usual symptoms of nostalgia. Many no longer looked to the future for their motoring needs, preferring to wallow unashamedly in the past. The loss of the air-cooled VW was mourned by all those who had come to know and love it. The classic VW era had ended.

As a result of this innovation, a huge new industry developed on both sides of the Atlantic, to cater for people who wanted to continue to use and enjoy the classic Splitties, Bays and Wedges. Independent companies began to manufacture spare parts for all three models, and restoration companies began to thrive, to the point where it became possible to obtain virtually every component necessary to keep old Buses in good running order.

From Volkswagen's perspective, it would have been foolhardy to continue to produce vehicles powered by the air-cooled flat-four. The company had spent more than forty years developing and perfecting the engine. Millions of the alloy units had been used, not only in the Bus, Beetle, Karmann Ghia and Type 3 and 4 saloons, but also in light aircraft, boats and industrial applications throughout the world. It had been one of the automotive industry's most successful engines, whose use had spanned more than half of the twentieth

The tailboard and sideflaps have been removed to emphasize this double-cab's truck styling.

century. However, all good things must come to an end, and when it came to footing the wages bill at the factory, not even Volkswagen could afford to be sentimental.

The 1600 and 2-litre engines had simply run out of steam. They did not produce sufficient power and were too fuel-thirsty to cope with the demands of the 1980s. They were also no match for the opposition. In Britain, the evergreen Ford Transit was cheaper to buy, cost less to run and repair, and could carry the same number of people or cargo, at higher speeds. In Italy, the Fiat Amigo – the 'baby' VW Transporter – was air-cooled, and a much smaller vehicle, but sold well because it was extremely inexpensive both to buy and

Not even the single-cab Pick-Up is safe from devotees of radically lowered suspension.

to run. In Germany, Daimler-Benz's commercial range had powerful diesel engines (the cylinder blocks for which, incidentally, were made from the excess metal used in saloon-car engine production), which used half the amount of fuel consumed by a conventional petrol unit. Volkswagen were impelled to take the diesel route.

From 1982, the Wedge was powered either by a 1.9-litre water-cooled flat-four petrol engine, or a 1.6-litre diesel. The diesel was an in-line four, which had previously seen service in the Golf hatchback, but had been de-tuned for use in the Transporter. Developing 50bhp at 4,200rpm, it was no more powerful than the old 1600cc air-cooled engine, but the diesel brought the benefits of higher torque over a wider rev range, and much better fuel efficiency.

Being compact and inclined at an angle of 50 degrees, the diesel engine fitted into the tail-end of the Wedge without the need for bodywork modifications. However, being 200lb heavier than the air-cooled unit, it produced a considerable rear weight bias, despite the weight of a radiator and associated plumbing up front. Consequently, there was an adverse effect on handling. *Safer Motoring* tested one of these vehicles in December 1982, and the writer of the report commented that 'overall, the diesel was not quite as brisk as the conventionally powered van, itself not renowned for performance, but redeemed itself by its very smoothness'.

With 50mph achieved from rest in a minimum of 23 seconds, the 'oil burner' was slow, and it was still necessary to make heavy use of the gears to get the best out of the engine. However, as *Safer Motoring* pointed out,

Buyers of a diesel van are not looking for performance; their wish is economy. Volkswagen introduced the diesel version of the Transporter not for the private owner but for

Without its VW roundel and bright trim, the Bay's simple lines are enhanced. Note that the fresh-air grille has been 'blanked off' to give a smoother frontal appearance.

the business user. The payback with a diesel comes not on long hauls, where the vehicle is running at relatively high speeds, but in the stop-start of town deliveries with a large proportion of low-speed work and idling.

In the past, the traditional air-cooled 1600 engine proved itself capable of overall fuel consumption of around 25mpg (11.3l/100km). The 2-litre version was good for 21mpg (13.5l/100km), whereas the diesel never returned less than 28mpg (10l/100km). A figure of 38mpg (7.45l/100km) was easily attainable in motorway driving conditions.

As well as providing businesses with much lower operating costs, the diesel-engined Camper conversions also reduced the cost of family holidays. Volkswagen had pulled it off yet again. A number of traditional customers might have turned their attentions elsewhere, but a whole new generation was quickly discovering the advantages of owning a well-built people or cargo carrier.

The water-cooled Wedges lasted in production for seven years, before being replaced by a wholly new Transporter which, in terms of design, would turn conventional Volkswagen Bus thinking on its head.

THE PRESENT DAY

In 1989, Volkswagen launched the fourth generation of Transporters. Officially the Type 4 (not to be confused with the Type 4 saloon of the 1960s and 70s), this model not only had a water-cooled engine, but it was transversely mounted in the front, and drove the front, rather than the rear, wheels. For Volkswagen, it was a U-turn of mammoth proportions.

The range was as comprehensive as ever, with all the variants of the previous models, and to a striking design. The Nordhoff philosophy of a box on wheels had not changed, but this was a much larger box – in short- and long-wheelbase guises – with much more internal space, and a cargo or passenger area with a flat floor by courtesy of the front-mounted engine. There were large double doors at the rear, and an even bigger sliding side door, all of which again improved access to the interior. To reduce aerodynamic drag, the front of the vehicle was steeply raked, and the traditional circular headlamps – a strong styling feature of the Transporter from the Splittie prototypes of 1949 – were gone, perhaps for good. In their place were roughly oblong units designed in the contemporary Japanese style. A VW roundel was placed in the centre of the radiator grille. It was essential for marque identification, as this was arguably the first Bus that was not instantly recognizable as a VW. Naturally, reactionaries reckoned it to be characterless.

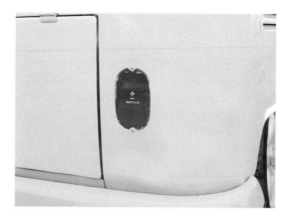

Attention to detail – the tail-lamps have been made flush with the bodywork, in a typical Cal-look touch.

For Volkswagen, the new Transporter that would take the company to the end of the twentieth century and beyond made a lot of sense. The radical design was a means of consolidating and rationalizing the entire range. The passenger cars, whether Volkswagen or Audi, were all front-engined, front-wheel drive (apart from Syncros and Quattros), so it was only natural that the Transporter should have been brought into line, as a way of easing production problems and reducing costs.

It may lack character, but the fourth-generation Bus is the safest and most sophisticated of the breed to date. The unitary-construction body has integrated 'crumple' zones, to absorb shock more easily in the event of a collision, while ABS braking and airbags add to the safety package today.

The move in engine position from the rear to front led to a marked loss of traction, particularly on loose or damp surfaces, but Volkswagen could respond to the critics. Through market research, they knew that the majority of customers never took their vehicles to places where good traction was critical. For the minority who did venture into sticky terrain, Volkswagen had an answer – the four-wheel drive 'Syncro' option was made available.

Technically advanced, Syncro is a 'part-time' four-wheel drive system in which the rear wheels are driven only when electronic gadgetry senses a loss of traction. The advantage of this over a permanent four-wheel drive system is that, during normal driving conditions, when the front wheels only are propelling the vehicle, fuel is not being wasted by the additional driving of the rear wheels.

The biggest improvement occurred under the bonnet. For years, journalists and owners had voiced discontent at the Transporter's relative lack of power and performance. They had a point. Conducting one of the old air-cooled models up a steep hill on a crowded motorway could be an uncomfortable experience – although it might be part of the vehicle's character.

A range of engines was eventually made available, which included a 1.9-litre 68bhp turbo diesel, a 2.5-litre 102bhp diesel capable of returning over 40mpg, and a torquey 2.4-litre 75bhp 5-cylinder diesel. In addition, there were 2.0 and 2.5-litre petrol units, and the magnificent 2.8-litre 140bhp V6 petrol engine, capable of rowing the top-of-the-range Caravelle people carrier along at speeds in excess of 130mph (210km/h). This Volkswagen had become one of the world's fastest, most powerful, quietest and most efficient people transporters.

A Cal-look dashboard that includes smoothed-off metalwork, and colourful instruments to match the upholstery.

The Volkswagen had also become a very expensive commodity. The company had long since taken the decision to pitch the range further upmarket and, despite the devastating effects of economic slumps, particularly in Western Europe during the 1980s and 90s, the German giant remained on top. And it is likely to stay there in the foreseeable future.

When Ben Pon and Ivan Hirst started the Transporter story back in the late 1940s, neither could have foreseen that the Bus would be such a huge success. It was the first vehicle ever of its kind, and each generation of it attracted new enthusiasts all over the world. Today, Transporters of all ages are big business. Although many examples have been scrapped, survivors will often be the deserving subject of a lengthy and expensive restoration – stunning examples of the marque.

Splitties and Bays have become highly prized by collectors everywhere. These immortal vehicles now command a greater following than at any time during the past, which shows no signs of abating.

NOT THE END

Volkswagen's plant at Puebla in Mexico is something of an oddity. Beetles and Bay-Window Buses were produced here for many years, and the original Beetle still is. It is Mexico's cheapest automobile, and provides transport for all but the country's poorest inhabitants. The Mexican government insists on its continued production for this reason, and their deal with the people in Wolfsburg is simple: stop Beetle production at Puebla, and you can leave Mexico altogether.

Production of the Bay-Window Bus continued alongside the Beetle until 1998. But even this was not the end. Volkswagen has

The colour co-ordinated cooling 'tinware', fan shroud and dynamo pedestal complement perfectly the chromed dynamo pulley and alloy crankshaft power pulley.

now launched, in 1998, the new Beetle – the first Volkswagen *officially* to bear the name. The new design is thoroughly modern, but with 'retro-styling' from the original Beetle. It is an important vehicle for the company's future prosperity, and the early indications are that it will sell in very large numbers.

The new car is being produced at the Mexican factory alongside the traditional Beetle, while production of the Bay-Window Bus has been transferred to the Brazilian plant. Experts had predicted that production of

A unique front-opening door; in case it flies open by accident, there is also a specially converted hearse.

A lot of hard work went into making this Bay handle like a pig.

the new Beetle would see the end of the traditional air-cooled Bus and Beetle, but this does not now seem likely. Others have argued that it is only a matter of time before Volkswagen comes to its senses, and starts to import air-cooled Beetles and Buses into Europe. This has not happened either, and never will. The Bays and Beetles are wildly out of date, and would not sell in sufficient quantity.

In 1989, well-known Barbados-born VW enthusiast Peter Stevens began manufacturing Beetles in Britain from new parts imported from Mexico, and 'new old stock' from Germany. The cars were built to a high specification by hand, on a purpose-built jig of unique design. They were of exceptional quality, with partially galvanized bodies to protect against corrosion, and fitted with the latest fuel-injected 1600cc catalytic converter engines from Mexico.

Complete with its smart sports wheels and bright red paintwork, the prototype was displayed in the showrooms of a Worcestershire-based Volkswagen dealer. Reaction from the car-buying public during the course of several weeks was interesting. People flocked to

Nice face, shame about the legs …

Will Volkswagen ever make a Bus with a 'retro Splittie' look? It's happened with the Beetle ...

see it; the car brought an affectionate smile to every face, they complimented it on its looks and, for those who had owned Beetles of yesteryear, it brought on serious feelings of nostalgia. But it did not sell.

When it came to a choice between a modern Volkswagen and the 'old' Beetle, those who could afford it went for a Golf or Polo. The modern cars are more comfortable and spacious, quieter, faster, and more economical. With a hatchback, they are also more convenient.

Why would Volkswagen want to produce a new car at the end of the twentieth century, based on the one it has been trying to get rid of for so long? The answer has implications for the fifth generation of Transporters. Modern vehicles, for all their convenience and

design brilliance, are aesthetically dull, and all tend to look the same. In the past five years or so, manufacturers have noted the unstoppable success of the classic-car movement. It has been responsible for the growth of a multi-billion dollar industry, which only once – in 1989 – dipped into recession (and bounced back pretty quickly). Those who spend a fortune restoring classics are usually the first to admit that their car has appalling brakes, dreadful fuel consumption and wild handling characteristics, but still they would not be without it.

Old classics are perceived to have style. They look fabulous. And this style overrides any considerations about their disadvantages in comparison with modern cars. The BMC Mini, for example, originally launched in 1959, is held in great affection by the British, the Japanese and other Europeans. Even a good restored or original example has an awful driving position, dismal performance and horrendous engine noise. But they look wonderful, and evoke memories of the Monte-Carlo rallies of the mid-1960s, when the cheeky little car was all-conquering.

Aware of the appeal of the classic style, manufacturers are beginning to produce vehicles that are modern and safe in every way, but designed to look like classics of old. Examples of this include the new Beetle, the Porsche Boxster, with its styling from the 1959 RSK two-seater Le Mans car, and the BMW Z3, which has body features clearly based on the 507 sports car built at Munich between 1955 and 1959. BMW – now owner of the Rover Group – is also on the brink of launching a new Mini for the twenty-first century; all the signs are that it will draw heavily on the styling characteristics of the original car, and it is likely to succeed commercially as a result.

The people at Volkswagen are perfectly aware of the enormous interest around the world in the classic air-cooled Transporters. A pristine Samba Splittie, put up for sale at

Immortal, visible and forever, the VW is the enduring classic 'bus' of the twentieth century.

any one of the hundreds of classic VW meetings held in the United States, will quickly fetch a hefty sum of money – up to 35,000 US dollars – and the Bus will probably be on its way to Japan without further ado.

It is almost inconceivable that the fifth-generation Transporters will not borrow heavily from the Split-Screens of the 1950s and 60s. Are those well-known features – a Y-shaped swage line and large VW roundel on the front panel, a peak above the windscreen, circular headlamps, retro-look dashboard and instruments, and wrap-around rear windows – poised to make a comeback?

It is impossible to improve upon perfect styling and perfect design, but, where automobile design is concerned, a few hidden treasures of the past may be about to be rediscovered. History may repeat itself, only this time the bad parts will be left out. By the middle of the twenty-first century, maybe the Bus will have turned through a full circle. Crash-test research in recent times has revealed that the safest place for a vehicle's engine, from a passenger's point of view, is in the rear. Horizontally opposed engines are inherently better-balanced, and reduce a vehicle's centre of gravity more effectively than conventional configurations.

The deficiencies of front-wheel drive – wheelspin, torque steer and a lack of traction – are well known. Electronic devices designed to control these flawed characteristics are not as effective as manufacturers had hoped. Will Volkswagen and others, therefore, revert to rear-wheel drive? Many hope so.

All these questions will be answered in due course, but one or two things are certain. The nature of motoring will change radically during the next few years, and, whatever type of vehicle will answer our transportation needs during the next millennium, it is a safe bet that Volkswagen will, as usual, be leading the way.

Index